Invest Like Buffett

Learn the Investment Strategies that
Made Warren Buffett Rich

By
Bradley Adams

not engaging in the rendering of legal, financial, medical or professional advice. The content within this book has been derived from various sources. Please consult a licensed professional before attempting any techniques outlined in this book.

By reading this document, the reader agrees that under no circumstances is the author responsible for any losses, direct or indirect, which are incurred as a result of the use of information contained within this document, including, but not limited to, errors, omissions, or inaccuracies.

Table of Contents

Introduction

For the past 36 years, the stock prices of Berkshire Hathaway have increased by 27%. Berkshire Hathaway, a multinational conglomerate owned by Warren E. Buffett, has been profitable and consistent.

If you asked Buffet to advise you on how a private investor like you could recreate his effective investment techniques, he would guide you to purchase stocks in Berkshire Hathaway. An extraordinarily smart and savvy businessman, this is a no-brainer. But if you purchase, or plan to purchase, other stocks single-handedly, perhaps through a managed investment trust or one at a time, studying Buffett's strategies is beneficial.

What about doing the most practical thing such as investing all your money in Berkshire Hathaway stock? This is not feasible for two reasons: One, since Buffett is an insurance expert, it is predominantly an insurance holding company. Because of this, the stock is nonexistent in many aspects of the stock industry such as health care and technology. Two, Berkshire has grown to have insurmountable success. This success can be compared to increasing the weight carried by the best horse in a race. Simply put, it might be more effective for you to do it on your own. Why? First, your investments are smaller and flexible. Second, you may perform exceptionally well if you buy more stocks in areas that you understand such as technology, health care, banking, etc. Buffett calls this remaining in your "circle of competence." Buffett's friends own the business, The Sequois Fund, which holds 30 percent of its assets in Berkshire.

Although the regular investor can pick up a lesson or two from the expert, it is impossible for anyone to recreate Buffett's previous or future investment strategies. The most evident reason is that Buffett can afford to purchase companies outright, instead of small parts or divisions. Additionally, he performs takeover arbitrage, which happens when there is a merger -- he purchases the shares of one company or sells those of the other. Buffet also invests preference shares, precious metals, and bonds. Berkshire has a few investments in some companies and is also a member of the board of directors in these companies. The hardest thing for anyone to recreate is Buffett's special unit of expert investors across the country who do everything possible to keep him well informed about any company he is intent on purchasing.

Additionally, Buffett assures family-run businesses that they can continue operating the company as though nothing has changed, even after he buys them. This is impossible for an individual to recreate. Buffett is an extremely intelligent man — a math genius — who has spent a large part of his life fanatically studying businesses and their balance sheets. He has also been mentored by a few of the most dynamic and enterprising investment experts of our generation such as Benjamin Graham.

Let's put it this way, although attempting to copy the Williams sisters or Pete Sampras does not necessarily mean that you will end up at Wimbledon, you might learn a thing or two from any advice they dish out or by studying their daily routine and the various things they do to help them win tennis games.

Buffett has stated several times that it is easy to replicate his method. He buys potential businesses with dependable, shareholder-friendly management, especially when these businesses are in temporary distress and the price is favorable. Then he just waits.

An entire collection of books has been written on Buffett and his investment strategies and a myriad of online forums, websites, and yearly meetings are dedicated to discussing Buffett and his methodology — almost cultish in fashion. There is a Buffett "guidebook" filled with quizzes and critical thinking tools to help individuals invest in just like Buffet does. This book is not targeted at the expert investor or the Chartered Financial Advisors (CFA), it is mainly targeted at normal investors who are certain that this resource will improve their investment journey.

Truthfully, most of Buffett's investment techniques are very useful for the regular investor. His advice, which he has given amply, is easy and almost infallible. He only buys what he thinks are dependable stocks of companies that are extremely strong and unbeatable — companies that will certainly still be at the top of their industries a decade later. He limits his choices to stocks in sectors in which he is knowledgeable. He searches for all the information available, ranging from CEO personalities and quirks to the company's return on equity. He meticulously reviews his errors and promptly fixes them. Although his loyalty lies with the management and staff of the company he buys, his greatest loyalty is to his investors. For Warren Buffett, being a risk-taker is the most despicable thing one can do.

Furthermore, Buffett strives not to make the same errors made by ordinary investors, such as buying the most attractive stocks at the peak of their fame, selling any stock that drops temporarily, trying to be flexible by purchasing all kinds of stocks in a variety of industries, being tempted by intriguing tales without any actual proof of numbers, and stubbornly clinging to his losses while unwarily making profits off his winnings by selling them.

Simply put, as Buffett has said, his success can mainly be attributed to his investments being reasonable and practical. To paraphrase this: Buffett invests with maximum, or even desperate, effort.

A word of caution: It is unnecessary for a regular investor to emulate every single technique used by Buffet, especially, his predilection for buying just a few stocks — a disastrous decision for someone who is not an expert on making multiple investments.

Chapter 1: The Real Warren Buffett

Warren Edward Buffett was born on August 30, 1930. His dad, Howard, was a stockbroker who went on to become a Congressman, and his mum, Leila, also has an eye for business. He was the second child and had two sisters. While still very young, he showed great tenacity for business and money.

Friends speak of his supernatural ability to calculate number columns spontaneously, a skill that still amazes Warren's present-day business counterparts.

As a six-year-old, Buffett paid 25 cents for six bottles of Coca-Cola at his grandfather's grocery store. He sold each bottle for one nickel and made a 5% profit. While other children his age were busy playing jacks and hopscotch, Warren was busy making money off his first "business" venture.

Buffett made his entry into the world of business five years after.

When he was 11, he paid $38 for three shares of Cities Service Preferred, he purchased these shares for himself and his elder sister, Doris. Shortly after he bought the stock, it dropped to about $27 for each share. A scared but assiduous Warren clung to his shares till the prices moved back up to $40. He sold them immediately — an error he later regretted as Cities Services rebounded up to $200. He learned an essential investment lesson from this experience: Do not overestimate the importance of patience.

Warren Buffett's Education

Buffett graduated from high school in 1947 at 17 years old. He didn't like the idea of going to college; as he had saved $5,000 (Almost $60,000 in today's money) which he made from delivering newspapers. His dad had different intentions, and under the compulsion of his father, he went to study at the Wharton Business School of the University of Pennsylvania.

He only spent two years at the University of Pennsylvania, stating he was more knowledgeable than most of his professors. Warren moved back home after the death of his dad, and transferred to University of Nebraska. Although he had a full-time job while in college, he graduated in just three years.

When it was time for graduate school, Buffet was just as adamant as he was a few years earlier. Eventually, he was convinced to apply at Harvard Business School, and in the worst admission error ever made, his application was rejected because he was too young. He felt insulted and submitted another application to Columbia where other acclaimed investors, such as David Bodd and Ben Graham, were professors, this experience completely changed the course of his life.

Ben Graham's Influence

Ben Graham became famous in the 1920s. At the time, the world regarded investment as "playing with fire." Graham looked for stocks that were cheap to the point that they had no risk at all. One of his famous investments was in the Northern Pipeline, an oil transportation corporation owned by the Rockefellers.

Although the stocks were sold at $65 per share, Graham studied the balance sheet and discovered that the organization had a bond worth $95 per share. He tried to sway the management to sell the company to him, but they rejected his offer. Just shortly after, he launched a tactical business strategy and earned a place on the Board of Directors. The company's bonds were sold, and a dividend of about $70 was paid.

Ben Graham was only 40 years old when he wrote *Security Analysis,* one of the best books ever written on the stock market. Then, the risks involved were too high; equity investments were laughable (there was a drop in the Dow Jones from 381.71 to 41.22 about three to four years after the famous 1929 crash).

Around this period, Graham developed the rule of "intrinsic" business value, which estimates the actual worth of business without considering the stock price at all.

The use of intrinsic value enables investors to determine the worth of a company and make the appropriate investment choices. The next book he wrote, *The Intelligent Investor*, which is revered by Warren who thinks of it as the "best book on investment that has ever existed," presented Mr. Market (the greatest investment analogy that has ever existed) to the world.

Because of his easy yet extensive investment principles, Ben Graham became an icon to Warren Buffett who was 21 years old at the time.

After reading an old publication of *Who's Who*, Warren discovered that Graham was the president of a small, unpopular insurance organization known as GEICO. On one Saturday morning, he boarded a train going to Washington D.C. in search of the head office. Getting there, the doors were closed. He persevered and continued knocking on the door until it was opened by a janitor. He then asked if anyone was available.

By a stroke of luck or fate, someone was. It happened that a man was still busy on the sixth floor. Upon meeting this man, Warren started inquiring about the company and its business operations, a discussion that lasted for four hours. The man was Lorimer Davidson, the Financial Vice President. This experience impacted Buffett throughout his life. Eventually, through his company Berkshire Hathaway, Buffett acquired GEICO. An excellent performer in his graduate studies at Columbia, no other student apart from Warren ever received an A+ in Graham's classes. Sadly, Ben Graham and Howard (Warren's father) discouraged Warren from working on Wall Street after his graduation. Not one to be deterred by anything, Buffett offered to work an unpaid internship for Graham's partnership, which Graham promptly declined as he wanted to employ Jews who were rejected at Gentile companies. Warren was devastated.

Back To His Hometown

After going back home, Buffett worked at his father's brokerage firm and he started dating a girl named Susan Thompson. Their relationship quickly became serious and they and got married in April 1952. They rented a three-room apartment where they paid $65 per month. It was a shabby apartment that was shared with a family of mice. This was where they had their daughter, Susie. In order to save money, they fashioned a bed for her out of their dresser drawer.

Over the course of these first years, Warren's investments were mainly restricted to some real estate and a Texaco station, but they were both unsuccessful. He taught night classes at the University of Omaha (this might have been impossible a few months before). In a bid to overcome his extreme fear of public speaking, he enrolled in a course by Dale Carnegie. Eventually, things changed for the better. One day, he got a call from Ben Graham inviting him to work for him. His highly anticipated opportunity finally came.

Working For Ben Graham

Warren and his wife relocated to the suburbs of New York. Most of his days were spent reviewing S&P reports in search of investment options. It was during this period that the disparities between Buffett and Graham's principles became evident. Warren developed an interest in the operations of a company; what made it better than other business rivals. Ben was concerned with the numbers, whereas Warren took interest in the management of the company before making an investment decision. Graham reviewed the investment statement and balance sheets and that was all, he had no interest in corporate management. Warren's personal capital moved up from a measly $9,800 to about $140,000 within 1950 and 1956. With this capital reinforcement, he readjusted his focus to Omaha and made new plans. Warren Buffett put together seven limited partners including his aunt, Alice, and his sister, Doris. They came up with $105,000. He included his own $100,000, formally establishing Buffett Associates,

Ltd. By the end of the year, the capital was about $300,000.

He had greater plans for that stack of cash. He paid $31,500 for a house that he fondly named "Buffett's Folly," and his partnerships were primarily managed from one of the bedrooms in his home. He later moved to a small office. By then, his life was beginning to take root: He had a beautiful wife, three kids, and a highly successful business.

In the course of the five years that followed, Buffett's partnerships recorded an exceptional profit of 251.0%, whereas the Dow had only increased by 74.3%. Although a mini-celebrity in his hometown, he never gave anyone investment tips despite persistent badgering from strangers and family members. By 1962, the partnership had a capital of more than $7.2 million, and Buffett's personal stake was $1 million. He charged no payment for the partnership. Instead, he had rights to one-fourth of the returns more than 4%.

In addition, he had more than 90 limited partners throughout the US. In a swift move, he merged them all into one entity called "Buffett Partnerships Ltd.," and increased the minimum investment to $100,000.

In 1962, Charlie Munger relocated from California back to where he grew up, Omaha. Although he was arrogant, he was all shades of brilliant. He didn't have a bachelor's degree, but still managed to attend Harvard Law School. A mutual friend introduced Munger and Buffett who instantly connected with each other. This was the foundation for a friendship and business partnership that would exist for the following forty years.

According to Karteri Drexler (in Icons of Business, 2007), ten years following its establishment, the assets of Buffett Partnership had increased by more than 1,000% in comparison to Dow's slightly more than 100%. As the founders of a company that had more than $45 million in assets, both Warren and Susie had personal stakes of $6,848,936. Like anyone would say, Buffett was set for life. In a smart move, just as he was achieving some level of success, Buffett decided that no new accounts would be accepted into Buffett Partnership At this time, the Vietnam war had begun and inflation had plagued the stock market. This inflation was championed by people who were absent when the depression took place.

As Buffett kept making his worries for the increase in stock prices known, the Buffett Partnership carried out the most successful coup of 1968, making over 59% profits, propelling the assets of the partnership well over $104 million. The following year, Warren did much more than move the money to newly opened accounts; he liquidated the company.

In May 1968, he expressed to his partners his fears about how it was impossible for him to get any bargains in the present market. Warren spent the rest of the year liquidating the business while excluding two companies - Diversified Retailing and Berkshire. The partners distributed the Berkshire shares among each other, with Buffett sending a letter to let them know that he will only be involved in part, and as such, will not be under any obligation to them in the years to come. However, because he had a stake of 29% of the shares at Berkshire company, he made his intention of holding on to his shares in the business. The reason wasn't clear.

Controlling Berkshire Hathaway

In the previous years, there was a clear definition of Warren's duties at Berkshire. On May 10, 1965, after amassing about 49% of the company's stake, Warren became the company director. Berkshire had almost collapsed because of incompetent management, and he was certain that a few minor adjustments would go a long way in improving management. Warren promptly named Ken Chace as the chairman of the company, granting him complete autonomy over the business. He chose not to issue him any stock options, however, as he felt it was unjust to shareholders. Instead, he decided to cosign a loan of $18,000 for his new company president to buy 1,000 units of shares in the company.

After two years, in 1967, Warren called Jack Ringwalt, the founder of National Indemnity and a major shareholder, for a talk. He asked Ringwalt his thoughts on the business worth. Ringwalt's answer: Value each share at a minimum of $50, an excess of $17 above the market price of about $33 then.

Right there, Warren paid $8.6 million to buy the entire company. Also that year, Berkshire paid dividends of 10 cents on all its unpaid stock — the only time this ever happened. According to Warren, the dividend was probably announced while he was in the bathroom. In 1970, Buffett announced his chairmanship of the Berkshire Hathaway Board, and this was the first time he penned a letter addressed directly to all shareholders. This was previously done by Ken Chace.

The president's discretion was evident in his capital allocation that year as well. Profits from textile were a meager $45,000; whereas, banking and insurance raked in $2.6 million dollars and $1.6 million dollars respectively. This mere sum gained from the barely successful textile mills in New Bedford, Massachusetts was the source of capital used to establish Berkshire Hathaway, making it one of the present-day business giants.

About one year later, he was given the opportunity to purchase an organization named "See's Candy." This gourmet chocolate maker didn't sell its candy to customers at the usual price of confectionary treats, in fact it sold candy at a much higher price.

The balance sheets confirmed what most Californians suspected, they had no problem with spending a little bit more for the exquisite "See's" flavor. The investor then made the choice that Berkshire would pay a cash down payment of $25 million for the company. The owners of See's Candy were intent on getting $30 million instead; however, they gave in soon enough. This was the most profitable investment ever made by Berkshire.

After numerous investments and an SEC investigation (after resulting in the failure of a merger), Munger and Buffett offered to buy the stock at Wesco at an inflated price, just because they felt it was the right direction to follow at that time — and as expected, the government doubted this. Buffett started noticing a steady rise in Berkshire Hathaway's net worth.

Between 1965 and 1975, the stock value of the company rose from $20 to about $95. It was during this time that Warren bought the last of the Berkshire stocks. When the distribution was made among the partnership, he had a personal stake of 29%. Many years after, he had over $15.4 million as an investment in the company at about $32.45 for every share. This increased his stake to more than 43% of the stock. At this time, his wife, Susie, had ownership of about 3%. Everything he owned was put into Berkshire. Since he had no other form of personal holdings, the business became his only source of investment.

Buffett renewed his business relationship with GEICO in 1976. They had recorded incredibly high rate of losses, and their stocks dropped to $2 for every share. Warren smartly discovered that the business was still functional, and the majority of the issues were caused by an incompetent management team.

During the following years, Berkshire regained its stand in the failing business and gained millions in profit. By September that year, Ben Graham, who never let go of his investment in the business, died a few months prior to the turnaround. In the years that followed, GEICO would later become a subsidiary of Berkshire.

Turnaround In His Personal Life

Shortly after this period, a life-altering and disturbing event took place in Buffet's life. Susan Buffett separated from him. She was forty-five years old at the time. Though they were still married, Susie, who was a singer and humanitarian at the time, relocated to San Francisco, demanding to live alone. This was disastrous for Warren as Susie had been there for him all through his life. They were still close, spoke with each other every day, joined their children for the Christmas family gathering at their beach house in California, and went on their yearly trip to New York.

Being separated from Susan made life difficult for Buffett, but he eventually adapted to this change. Numerous women were contacted by Susie who asked them to go on a date with Warren. She finally set up Warren with a waitress named Astrid Menks. With Susie's support, after about a year, Astrid moved in with Buffett.

Investments Outside Berkshire

Warren had become so famous by the late 70s that even the slightest speculation that he would purchase a stock caused the prices of the stocks to increase by up to 10%. Berkshire Hathaway stocks were selling at more than $290 per share, and Buffett's net worth was about $140 million. Paradoxically, Warren never sold any stake in his business, meaning that the only cash he had was his salary of $50,000. It was around this time that he told another investor, "All my money is in Berkshire. I want some nickels outside."

This was a motivation for Warren to expand his investment. He decided to start investing for his personal life. From the book *Buffett*, written by Roger Lowenstein, Buffett took greater risks than he did with Berkshire. One time, he purchased copper futures that were unfounded speculations. Within a short period, he had started making profits amounting to $3 million. When a friend urged him to diversify into real estate, Buffet answered: "When the stock market is so simple, what's the point of buying real estate?"

Charity Plans By Berkshire Hathaway

Later, Buffett displayed his knack for going against the trend. In 1981, otherwise known as the decade of greed, Berkshire declared a plan for a charity that he approved, although it was formulated by Munger. The plan involved the allocation of $2 for every Berkshire stock owned by a shareholder to specific charities.

This was a popular processes on Wall Street. The CEO would typically select the people to receive hand-outs from the company -- they would usually go to other organizations, churches, and executive schools. This plan was very successful and over the years caused a steady increase in the price of each share. Eventually, Berkshire shareholders were giving away millions of dollars yearly, for their own cause.

After a backlash at The Pampered Chef, one of Berkshire's subsidiaries, the program stopped. The backlash was caused by Buffett's decision to assign his portion of the charity event to some controversial pro-choice charities. In 1982, another significant thing happened: Stock prices increased to $750 per share. The majority of this profit was due to Berkshire's stock portfolio, which had an estimated worth of more than $1.3 million.

Strange Investment Style

Despite all the exceptional businesses Berkshire acquired, the best was yet to come. Warren Buffett visited Nebraska Furniture Martin in 1983, this was multi-million-dollar furniture business set up by Rose Bumpkin, fondly called Mrs. B by local residents. He spoke to Mrs. B. and inquired if she would like to sell the business to Berkshire Hathaway. She simply responded with a "Yes," and sold the business for $60 million. A simple handshake closed the deal and a single-page contract was written. The paper was nonchalantly kept away by the Russian-born immigrant who didn't check it until several days after getting the letter.

In 1984, Berkshire acquired a company known as Scott & Fetzer. The company was under a hostile takeover when a local purchase order was submitted by the Chairman, Ralph Schey. Ivan Boesky, an American stock trader, made a counterproposal of $69 per share, the initial offer was $50 per share, and this was $5 higher than the market price.

There was great apprehension in Scott & Fezer — manufacturers of the World Book encyclopedia and Kirby vacuum cleaners. Buffett owned about 25% of a million shares and he called them to propose a merger. They called back almost instantly, and Berkshire proposed $60 for each share in solid cash. Less than one week after, upon closure of the deal, Berkshire had acquired another $315 million-dollar money-making power company. The limited cash outflow from a barely successful textile loom had helped in building one of the biggest businesses globally. The following decade came with even more success. There would be a rise in Berkshire shares from $2,600 to almost $80,000 during the 90s. In 1986, Buffett paid $850,000 for a pre-owned Falcon aircraft. As Buffett's popularity continued to grow, it was difficult for him to comfortably board commercial planes. It was hard for him to adapt to this luxurious way of living, but he was extremely fond of the jet. In the 90s, his love for jets partially led him to buy an executive jet. The 90s continued with a steady rise in the value of Berkshire and, as expected, the only problem was the stock market crash in 1987. The fluctuation in the market had no effect on Warren and he cooly looked at the price of his company and resumed business. This was his impression of stocks and businesses and a deviation from the popular "Mr. Market" analogy. It was difficult and about 25% of Berkshire's market capital was swept away.

Warren continued, undisturbed as usual.

His Coke Adventure

The following year, 1988, Buffett overzealously began purchasing stocks in Coca-Cola. His former neighbor, who was the president of Coca-Cola at the time, observed an increase in the purchase of the shares and became worried. After investigating the purchase, he discovered that they were being bought from the Midwest.

Instantly, he suspected Buffett and he called him. Warren admitted to being responsible, and he asked that there should be no further discussions until he was lawfully permitted to reveal his holdings at the 5% limit. Within the months that followed, Berkshire had bought $1.02 billion of stock, which made up about 7% of the company. In the next three years, Buffett's Coca-Cola stock was more valuable than Berkshire in its entirety as at the time when the investment was made.

The Solomon Scandal

Berkshire Hathaway was now selling at $8,000 per share by 1989. Then, Buffett's individual net worth was over $3.8 billion. During the next decade, his net worth would grow to ten times this value, but there was a lot to overcome before this happened.

The Turn Of The Millennium

In the remaining months of the 90s, Berkshire stocks skyrocketed to as high as $80,000 a share. In spite of this extraordinary achievement, the Internet craze began, and Warren was said to have "fallen from his high place." Berkshire recorded a net profit of 0.5% for every share in

1999, and numerous publications were released on the fall of the "Oracle of Omaha." With absolute certainty that the reign of technology was temporary, Warren kept doing what he did best: assigning capital to companies that were selling lower than the intrinsic value. He reaped the rewards of his efforts. By the time the markets became more reasonable, Warren had regained his iconic status. Berkshire's stocks went back up to its incredible levels after plummeting to about $45,000 a share. The man from Omaha was once again regarded as an investment legend.

Chapter 2: The Circle Of Competence

"Being an expert on every company or too many companies is unnecessary. You just need the ability to assess companies using your circle of competence. The size of the circle is not really relevant; although, understanding its limits is important." (Warren Buffet)

With regards to the investment market, Warren Buffett is determined to remain with companies that are in his "circle of competence," this implies that he must be knowledgeable about the business and he needs to be able to analyze it. Through this profound understanding of the business, it was possible for him to accurately predict the performance of the business in the future. Like Buffett had said in the past, "You do not take a risk when you do not understand what you're doing." Therefore, by remaining within his circle of competence, the possibilities of risks were removed.

Within his circle of competence, Buffett knows the applicable laws with regards to capital allocation. He can make decisions. Additionally, he can exactly locate the source of his errors and adjust the principles of his decisions if required. Thus, Buffett's circle of competence provides him with that sense of control that is desired by everyone in a world that seems so uncertain, and this is what a lot of CEOs discovered after following their more typical investment strategies.

Buffett is famous for his perspicacity with regards to the management, price, competitive advantage, and understanding, which he attributes to the factors above. He seems to carry out his research and either acts right away or remains inactive, while being emotionally detached. Although it is true that Buffett's competitive advantage in capital management is not due to his objectiveness, but being emotionally intelligent and practicing both emotional stability. Emotions are necessary considerations when making decisions. They are vital to the process, particularly in the risky and enterprising decisions that Warren Buffet was brilliant at. They only disrupt the ability to make rational decisions when they overpower rationale.

As a human who is responsible for capital allocation, stability is key. Every decision taken by Warren is taken from a position of complete psychological assurance — something his circle of competence plays a key role in. Although he has also made all the necessary preparations in advance to ensure he agrees with the possibilities provided by the managing capital inside this circle and in accordance with its direction. Buffett's emotional stability is what provides him with the objectiveness that encourages and maintains his unique approach to capital management, making him better than a regular person.

Buffett would rather take decisions pertaining to his capital allocation within the scope of what is important and understandable. This is his zone of genius. Simply put, where he delightedly strikes his bat on the pitches that were thrown to him. It encompasses a world where he can objectively evaluate the opportunities available to him, a world where the factors considered while making his decisions are so evident that it is almost possible for him to touch them, and where he is so certain of them that he can definitely eliminate any doubts.

As a way of attaining this level of knowledge, Buffett draws his circle according to these steps:

1. He validates his knowledge by assessing the truths, the dynamics involved, and the relationship between them.

2. He makes sure that he formulates a reversal of the process, which enables him to confute his previous conclusions.

3. He assesses his knowledge by searching for feedback from the outcomes of his decisions.

Warren Buffett regards himself as a business expert, not a market expert, not a macroeconomic expert, and not even as a security expert.

Because of this, when Buffett started his investment journey, he researched all the companies that publicly traded securities in the United States -- he began with A and proceeded to the last letter of the alphabet, Z.

Progressively, during his analysis, Buffett formulated the mental images that would help him organize all that he was learning.

Therefore, while he recognizes that every business is subject to modifications over time, he has made it known that in the scope of the business analyst, there are definite truths that are applicable and expected to remain long-term, even in complicated systems as well.

Buffett's circle of competence is constructed within those companies and sectors that he was certain of identifying, understanding, and predicting the dynamics present in his truths.

As it is expected, he limits this idea of the important and comprehensible to the simple. He believes that the discovery may appear unjust, but in investments and businesses, higher profits are made by going along with the simple and evident rather than going with the complex, which might be hard to solve. Though Buffett confirmed that there have been improvements in his initial mental model, the size of his circle of competence with respect to the businesses he regards as valuable, have remained the same even as it was in his early years. This demonstrates the invariability of the principles of business economics.

Because of the increase in his knowledge that followed, Buffett aggressively protected the boundaries of his circle, given the impact of human behavior on these elements. Warren learned all these lessons as he made his way from a rookie investor to the capital manager and eventually, investment legend.

Chapter 3: Buffett And The Influence Of People In His Life

"I really like teaching. I've been doing it formally and, you could say, somewhat informally all my life, and I certainly had the greatest teachers you could imagine. So if somebody thought that I did a decent job at teaching, I'd feel very good about that." (Warren Buffet)

Like a lot of iconic people, it would have been impossible for Buffett to attain such levels of success without the people around him. Most of Buffett's achievements were influenced by a lot of important people in his life and the relationships he built.

Howard Buffett

Warren's father, Howard Buffett, influenced him from a very young age. Howard was the owner of a brokerage firm. As a child, Warren was often seen around the business, placing stock prices on a big board, emulating his father's trade. Warren visited the New York Stock Exchange when he was 10, and by 11, he purchased three shares of Cities Service Preferred, which were his first stocks.

Benjamin Graham

The acclaimed pioneer of modern value investing, Benjamin

Graham's impact on Buffett is evident in most of the investment decisions made by Buffett. Buffett knew about Graham after reading his book, *The Intelligent Investor*, in his final year at the University of Nebraska. He went on to study at Columbia University where he was taught by Graham. He graduated with a master's in economics; after graduating, Warren became interested in carving his niche in Wall Street and he reached out to Graham, who was a member of GEICO's Board of Directors. Although, Graham declined his request even after Warren offered to work without payment. Later, he was called back and employed by his mentor; after which he started formulating his brilliant investment techniques.

Charlie Munger

Buffett's closest business associate was from Omaha as well. Charlie Munger became an investor after enrolling in Harvard Law without an undergraduate degree and later joined Buffett's company. Although Munger had other successful businesses, he is recognized as a co-host of the organization's popular annual shareholder meetings, and the vice chairman of Berkshire Hathaway. Also, as a result of Munger's impact, the new partnership brought in profits of 1,156% within the first decade, in comparison with Dow's 122.9% increase.

Susan Buffett

Buffett discloses that his second-best teacher is his first wife, Susie Buffett. He says she helped him learn so much about the investment market.

In the book, *Becoming Warren Buffett*, he gives Susie credit for helping him get in touch with his emotional side.

He says, "I was twisted, and she straightened me out."

They were married until Susan's death in 2004. Prior to her death, she was the 17th richest woman in the world, serving as the chairman of the Buffett Foundation. She was also a director of Berkshire Hathaway.

Buffet says, having an understanding partner is very beneficial. This is even more evident in marriage. He considers this the most life-changing decision to ever take. His thinks even though you are not responsible for how you were born and trained, you are responsible for who you decide to marry. Marriage is the ultimate partnership and your choice of partner would significantly affect your happiness and success. He said he lucked out in these areas.

"Attaining this level of success is more enjoyable with a partner and this is unquestionable." (Warren Buffet)

Astrid Menks

Though Buffett keeps his personal life private from the public eye, his relationship with Astrid and his wife is widely known. Buffett and Susie separated in 1977, though they remained legally married. Before the separation, she implored her friend, Astrid Menks, to care for him. This was the beginning of a long-term relationship between Warren and Astrid, with the full blessings of Susie. The trio exchanged joint Christmas cards yearly. Buffett and Susie remained married until she passed away from cancer in 2004. In 2006, Astrid and Buffett married.

Alice Schroeder

The book titled *The Snowball, Warren Buffett and the Business of Life*, was Buffett's biography, written by Alice Schroeder. The biography provided a peek into the life of the private billionaire. In addition to Schroeder's Wall Street grounding, she was also the only stock analyst Buffett spoke to and this made her the perfect biographer for the investment legend. She was with him for more than 2,000 hours as he told her all the details of his life. In spite of Buffett's demands that she write all the details truthfully, that she tell the truth without any prejudice, he was unhappy with how he was represented in the book. Following the book's publication book, he disassociated himself from Schroeder.

Chapter 4: Right Temperament Of A Successful Investor

In the 2003 report of Berkshire Hathaway's shareholder meeting, the two great investors, Charlie Munger and Warren Buffett were asked to explain the temperament of a successful investor. According to Munger, an investor must own stocks for as long as possible without fretting. Buffett buttressed this assertion by adding that successful traders keep calm at all times, irrespective of the direction and volatility of the market.

He stressed that overly focusing on the price of stocks is a form of submissiveness to the market. A trader must focus on the value as much as the price and must be ready to buy more if the particular stock he has bought goes up.

Furthermore, Buffett stated that your ability as an investor to concentrate on one or two stocks in a year can make you a fortune. The key to success is to get it right a few times and avoid incurring big losses.

Munger expressed surprise that most big investment organizations make the mistake of analyzing too many stocks rather than focusing on only a few potentially profitable stocks.

The following logical points can be summarized from the afore-stated pieces of advice from the two businessmen:

- Focus more on value than price so as to outperform the average investor and achieve success in the market.

- Focus on one or two stocks in a year. Never try to analyze and evaluate every single stock in the market.

- Tame your emotion. Analyze logically and not emotionally; employ courage and confidence.

How Warren Buffett Became A Genius

The right temperament is the most significant factor that accounted for Buffett's business and investment success. His ability to keep his emotions at bay is a key factor in his successful achievements. The majority of people are amazed at his ability to appropriately value an investment. In fact, Buffett uses the same investment calculation model and business insights that are available to the average investor. What distinguishes Buffett from others is his self discipline and the resolve to stick to his investment principles regardless of the condition of the market.

The aforementioned attributes do not portray him as stubborn and rigid to the ever-changing market dynamics, however. What makes him a genius is that he maintains the same temperament and remains unperturbed by the prevailing environment.

It is worthy of repetition that in the world of investment, temperament takes precedence over financial knowledge. Numerous brokerage reports and chat group discussions are major sources of distractions. Note that most investment ideas are simple and easy to understand.

It must, however, be noted that the ability to control one's temperament is not Buffett's only asset; there are other major factors that contribute to his success as an investor and a businessman.

In-depth knowledge, powerful business insights, and accumulated experience have also added to his circle of competence. Advanced mathematics nor the ability to evaluate every business is not a prerequisite to a successful business. Rather, hard work and years of experience are notable factors.

Chapter 5: Value Investing World

According to Warren Buffett, successful traders are self-dependent. You need to shut your ears and shun the analyses and recommendations made by talking heads on the television or newspapers. Never be a pushover. If you are unsure of an answer to a stock or business, walk away and try the next one.

It is worthy of repetition that in the world of investment, temperament takes precedence over financial knowledge. Numerous brokerage reports and chat group discussions are major sources of distractions while most investment ideas are simple and easy to understand.

Investing In Businesses

Forbes Magazine narratives made us believe that Warren Buffett made his fortune majorly from the stock market. While this is not entirely untrue, the fact is that Buffett acquired his fortunes mainly through his company, Berkshire Hathaway, and thereafter leveraged on its success to purchase other companies.

In other words, after successfully building Berkshire Hathaway, Buffett started selling shares to the public. Rather than merely investing in stocks, Buffett is more interested in acquiring businesses and turning them to fortunes.

Business intelligence is one of the topmost qualities needed to spot a good business. You need to be a business owner to acquire such intelligence, however. The above quality contributed to my regard for Warren Buffett as not only an investor but also an entrepreneur.

Guides To Running Your Investments Like A Business

Ensure you have an in-depth understanding of your business.

"Never invest in a business you can't understand." (Warren Buffet)

Warren Buffett's long-term experience in the financial services industry has contributed significantly to the successful management of his company, Berkshire Hathaway. He refused to invest in the technology industry at the advent of the dot com boom solely because of his lack of knowledge in technology.

"If you understood a business perfectly and the future of the business, you need very little in the way of a margin of safety."

Empower yourself with knowledge of numbers.

"Accounting is the language of business." (Warren Buffet)

Financial literacy is a must. You need to understand and

record every cash inflow and outflow of your business. Proper management of cash flow, which is the lifeblood of business, will ensure maximum control of your business. Warren Buffett equipped himself with knowledge of fiscal numbers to keep the company afloat even during the recession.

There is no complete business failure.

Berkshire Hathaway was a dead textile company when it was taken over by Warren Buffett. Rather than seeing the business as an absolute failure, Buffett saw in the company's subsidiaries what others could not see. He repositioned the company to become one of the most valuable companies in the world.

Again, there is no absolute business failure. It takes a deep insight to see the potential in a dying business and resuscitate it. However, it is worth reiterating that the knowledge of numbers is essential.

Management is vital to the sustenance of a business.

"When a management with a reputation for brilliance tackles a business with a reputation for a bad economy, it is the reputation of the business that remains intact." (Warren Buffet)

One of the key features Warren Buffett considers when buying a business is sound management. This is because, without competent management, the goal of an entrepreneur starting a business may remain unachieved.

"Somebody once said that when looking to hire people, look for three qualities; integrity, intelligence, and energy. If they don't have the first, the other two will kill you. You think about it; it's true. If you hire somebody without the first, you really want them to be dumb and lazy."

Know yourself.

"It takes 20 years to build a reputation and only five minutes to ruin it. If you think about that, you will do things differently." (Warren Buffet)

Integrity is an outstanding trait that I learned from going through the life history of Warren Buffett. Integrity goes beyond being honest; it cuts across every facet of life. Ask yourself: What is your guiding principle?

After taking a closer look at various companies in different sectors of the economy, I realized that a common feature found at the core of their business dealings is integrity. Integrity is not found as part of the core values of any business; rather, it has to be imbibed into the business by the entrepreneur or management.

In summary, you need to know yourself (you can't give what you don't have) and make integrity your watchdog. If you're a person of integrity, it will reflect in your business culture as well. Develop this fine quality and stick to it, let it guide you in all that you do, especially when you're doing business.

Be careful when selecting your business associates.

It is worthy of emphasis that Warren Buffett's choice of Charlie Munger as his long-term friend and close associate hugely contributed to his success.

A business partnership is analogous to a marital relationship. It can make or break a partnership as well as the business. It is imperative that you choose a positive-minded partner; someone who you can have an enduring friendship with and someone who contributes immensely to your self-improvement.

Plan for long term.

"Focus on your customers and lead your people as though their lives depend on your success." (Warren Buffet)

One reason most businesses fail to weather the storm is the myopic, short-term goal focus of either the management or the entrepreneur. One thing I've learned from Warren Buffett is the ability to project and make long-term plans. While still alive, he already laid down plans that will enable his successor at Berkshire Hathaway to have a smooth transition after his death.

As a smart businessman, Warren Buffett won't invest in any

business that lacks long-term plan, and this is one of the many reasons why he is a successful businessman. If you also wish to achieve success in your business, avoid investing in businesses that have no long-term goal.

Sadly, most entrepreneurs focus so much on making a profit, and they keep sucking every penny they make until the business drains funds without considering the long-term needs of the business. They continue to spend the profits until the business finally crashes. Smart entrepreneurs with a focus on the long-term survival of their business re-invest part of their profits into the business and take good care of their customers. Many successful businesses today have something in common, they make plans for, and continue working on their long-term goals.

Chapter 6: Bargaining The Market

"This is the cornerstone of our investment philosophy: Never count on making a good sale. Have the purchase price so attractive that even a mediocre sale gives good results." (Warren Buffet)

Buffett was always open about explaining his investment strategy, but he is always silent about his strategy on purchasing stocks. His strategy is more complex than it appears. Buffett buys stocks based on specific criteria, but occasionally he might decide to buy some that don't meet those criteria perfectly. Additionally, he is both a quantitative and qualitative investor who uses not just numbers and science but also art when buying stocks.

He had this guiding principle, however: Buy the stock or the entire company at a cheap enough price to create a "safety margin," so if the business fails, you won't lose so much. According to Benjamin Graham, the safety margin will cover up for part of your losses because there is provision for the possible eventuality.

Identifying and differentiating between an overpriced stock and a cheap one is not so easy. A couple of years ago, I was privileged to be shown a screaming bargain by a portfolio manager. It was the stock of a healthy company UST (formerly known as U.S Tobacco). At times, it takes an experienced investor or a professional portfolio manager to identify an incredibly "screaming bargain" with good numbers.

But one also must be careful because, at times, a seemingly screaming bargain could end up becoming a problem stock. So, sometimes you need to consider factors other than numbers before deciding on which stock(s) to buy.

Most investors buy several stocks that appear to be screaming bargains and pray they get it right, or at least make a decent profit from it. Although this may work out for some, at times, it doesn't.

Buffett didn't purchase his stock using such an approach, however. First, he conducts a background check to identify and differentiate the real screaming bargains in advance, rather than just trying his luck buying random stocks because they appear to be a screaming bargain. Even though there are lots of screaming bargains available in the market, Buffett always went for bargains that were sure to yield profit.

In the words of the poet Richard Wilbur, there are at least 13 ways of looking at a blackbird. So, there is no specific mathematical formula nor magical calculator that can be used to identify potentially profitable stocks, but there are some relatively simple screening criteria that Buffett used to identify a promising screaming bargain. Soon, we will discuss some simple screens that can help potential investors identify companies with promising potentials and the more screens scores a potential stock passes, the more potential such companies have to make a profit.

But then, what is this "screaming bargain" that Buffett was always talking about? In simple way, a screaming bargain refers to a cheap stock of a company that sells an ever-popular and high demand product and is financially healthy. Such a company must have a good reputation of employing talented researchers, brilliant salespeople, partnering with an excellent, splendid distribution chain, and be managed by capable hands.

In order to know whether a stock is cheap or not and to determine the financial health of a company, you need to check its earnings growth, book value, return on equity, the most recent cash flow, and the ratio of debt to equity. While all the potentials mentioned above are useful, none of them guarantees a surefire. This explains why it is imperative for a potential investor to be armed with enough information about the particular stock or industry he wishes to invest in beforehand rather than just focus on the numbers.

The Rules Of Thumb

Below are the most significant gauges of a company's potential and viability.

Companies that have a high and growing return on equity (ROE)

The term equity can be explained as a company's net worth in assets. To estimate the "return on equity," divide the equity into operating earnings, also known as net income. The net income is estimated after subtracting the preferred stock dividends.

ROE = net income/(ending equity + beginning equity/2)

The formula above is used to determine the ROE over a specific period (usually a year). From the formula above, the value of the company at the beginning of the period (or year) is added to the value at the end of the period (year). Then divide it by two to determine the average yearly value of that company.

Example:

ROE = £10,000,000/(£35,000,000 + £45,000,000/2), or 22.2%.

While doing your calculations, you need to be mindful of the numerator (the number on top) because there are various ways to estimate it. Buffett had a unique method of calculating the numerator. He would exclude the capital gains, yearly earnings, and all the losses from the company's investment portfolio, as well as any unusual bonus. Buffett would do this just to know how well the management was able to utilize the company's assets during what we might call an ordinary year.

From the results of a company's yearly ROE, you will be able to tell whether the management has been utilizing the company's assets efficiently and profitably.

According to Buffett, the most important way to test for the managerial economic performance is to check if the company achieves a regular high earnings rate on equity capital utilized, without the support of external leverage or other financial aid, rather than the accomplishments of consistent gains in earnings per share.

But then, why is "consistent gains in earnings per share" not the best criterion when trying to determine the financial health of a business or company? Because the company could decide to invest part of its earnings for the first year conservatively, for instance, in a deposit bank account, and use the profit for year two. It would then use the profits from year two toward year three, and the trend goes on. Each year, such companies will record earnings, right? Definitely, but at the end of the day, ROE would be determined by the bank deposit's rate of interest.

Another way some companies boost the figures is by borrowing or owing debts. Borrowing a large amount of money in order to invest will surely boost the equity-to-debt ratio of a company, thereby increasing its return. Not kosher recalls, Buffett always believed that "A good investment or business decisions will yield quite satisfactory financial results without the need for help via leverage."

It is important to note that Buffett wasn't entirely free from debt, however. Whenever there's a fine opportunity and he needs money to take advantage of such openings, he works towards it even if it means borrowing. According to Buffett, "If you wish to kill a rare bird always, walk around with your gun."

To boost ROE, according to Warren Buffett, a company could try to lower its taxes, borrow more money to expand or invest (at a lower interest rate, of course), sell off an unproductive division, lay off bottom-line employees (whose exit won't affect productivity) or buy another financially healthy company.

A company with a steady rise in ROE is a good pointer that can be used to estimate the financial health of such companies (especially if the ROE is high in comparison to its competitors).

Generally, an average ROE should fall between 10-20%. At

times, ROEs of certain industries could rise above 20% (which is quite impressive), but this could be due to certain variables such as a brisk economy. As companies expand, however, their ROE starts declining so companies with consistently high ROE are quite rare. Yet, high ROE means a higher stock price.

To obtain reliable data of various companies with their ROE, you can check websites such as Business.com, Investopedia, MSN MoneyCentral Investor, Entrepreneur, Inc.com, Value Line Investment Survey, and Standard & Poor's Stock Reports.

Companies with a consistent 15% growth in their earnings

Buffett was usually contented with a minimum of 15% compensation to cover the risk of inflation, the cost of paying taxes, and the general risks associated with the stock market. Simple speculations can help you determine whether a stock may compensate you with 15% or more yearly. Look out for:

- The current price;

- The earnings and growth rate in the past few years;

- Analysts' estimates on various financial websites.

(Note that the 15% return should include dividends).

At times, a growth in earnings could be misleading and give

rise to certain questions such as: If a company's revenue grew faster, does it mean that profits declined? Or did the earnings increase because of the sale of certain assets? What if the financial prosperity of the company is already reflected in the stock price? To clarify these, check the company's current price to earnings ratio, then compare it with those of its competitors' ratios, and finally compare it with its past price-to-earnings ratio.

Companies with high profit margins

When a company is well-managed, unnecessary costs will be cut down and this will lead to a rise in the profit margin of such company. You also need to be sure that such rise in profit margin is sustainable and not just a temporary or transient increase such as a drop in the price of raw materials such as ink, paper, courier fees, or a one-time tax write-off.

Although, some establishments have consistently high profit margins such as movie studios, others usually have relatively low margins such as retail stores.

Companies with consistently growing book value

Buffett would not begin his annual reports by stating how little or how much Berkshire's stock has risen, rather, he was known to always focus on talking about its "book value." That is, the company's worth per share, or what each shareholder would receive if Berkshire went bankrupt and the company was sold.

Ever since Buffett took over the management of Berkshire in 1965, the book value rose up by 24% per year. While the book value may not be the best scale of value, it is far better than relying on a stock's price, which is determined by the stock and bond market, investor psychopathology, and the economy.

According to Buffett, "The percentage rise (or fall) in the book value of any given year is likely a reflection of the change in the intrinsic value of that year."

Companies with a stable book value over the years are likely the old companies, such as the U.S. Steel company. Such companies have the best stock prices and are very stable, they are simply the best. Most companies with rising book value are the fast-growing companies, and their stock prices tend to rise simultaneously with the rise in book value.

One major way a company can boost its book value is by increasing its profits (by introducing new products or services or by cutting costs), purchasing potentially profitable companies, and having high returns on its equity. One peculiar feature of Berkshire is that its book value rises whenever the company's stocks increase in price.

One trick some companies use to boost their book value is issuing more shares, thereby diluting the value of current shareholders' stock.

Companies with little or no debt

A debt-equity ratio of 50% or lower is generally accepted as the industry standard (although many other measures are available). A sudden rise in the debt-equity ratio should be a cause for concern. Also, be watchful for a sudden spike in accounts payable bills that are yet to be paid.

Companies whose current cash flow shows that they are cheap compared to what they will be worth after the road

"The value of any business, bond or stock today is determined by the cash outflows and inflows — discounted at a decent interest rate — and this can be expected to occur all through the life of such an asset." (Warren Buffet)

What this means is that the worth of a business or security depends on the money it generates henceforth. The cash that you have at hand now is worth more than the cash in the future, hence, you can invest such cash in government bonds, which is safe and guaranteed. Also, reducing the value of the cash you might get in the future ("discount" it) by cutting down the interest rate on the money you did not receive. For instance, $10 in the next ten years from now might be worth paying just $7 based on the interest rate you chose.

The market value can be determined by a couple of variables such as the economic climate and investor's psychology among others. For instance, a closed-end mutual fund may sell for less than, more than, or exactly the expected worth of the assets (If such funds are traded like a stock, it could be used to purchase a variety of securities). Occasionally, such funds are sold at discounted prices, for reasons unknown.

To determine the intrinsic value of a particular stock, you need to first project the future cash flow of such company within the next few years, then decide how much you would pay for such a potentially beneficial stock today in order for cash to flow in the future.

Once you have estimated the value of a company and projected that the cash earnings are expected to rise fast, you will see that even if you purchase the stock at a high price, it will be worth the price. For instance, if the earnings of Coke were projected to rise at a 15% annual rate for the next fifty years, each $1 of the present earnings would rise to $1,083.65 in the next 50 years. Assuming a six percent discount rate is employed, the present intrinsic value would be estimated at $58.82, or about 59 times present earnings.

Buffett owned Coke a long time ago even when the p-e ratio was as high as 65.

If Coke's future earnings rise at a 15% annual rate, however, a 65% ratio may end up becoming a screaming bargain. If you do the math, you can tell how much the long term earnings growth would be worth — a lot.

Chapter 7: Admit Your Mistakes And Learn From Them

"Agonizing over errors is a mistake. But acknowledging and analyzing them can be useful, though the practice is rare in corporate boardrooms. There, Charlie and I have almost never witnessed a candid post-mortem of a failed decision, particularly one involving an acquisition . . . The financial consequences of these boners are regularly dumped into massive restructuring charges or write-offs that are casually waved off as "nonrecurring." Managements just love these. Indeed, in recent years it has seemed that no earnings statement is complete without them. The origins of these charges, though, are never explored. When it comes to corporate blunders, CEOs invoke the concept of the Virgin birth." (Warren Buffet)

One common and recurring title of the annual Berkshire reports is this: Even Buffett makes a lot of mistakes and he is never ashamed to admit his mistakes. For instance, in the 2000 annual report, while referring to the blunders he made in the past, he wrote: "I'm the fellow, remember, who assumed he knew the future economics of trading shoes, textiles, stamps, textiles, shoes, and second-tier department stores." Among the good attributes of a talented investor is the ability to humbly admit your mistakes and learn from them. Now, let's look at how Buffett admitted some of the mistakes he made in the past:

- As found in the annual report of 2000, Buffett admitted that the previous year, he told them that by advertising at GEICO in 2000, they would get their money's worth, but he was wrong. He continued that the extra cost they incurred did not produce an equivalent rise in demand. In addition, the percentage of inquiries that they later converted into sales dropped for the first time in many years. All these negative developments made the company make some adjustments to its per-policy acquisition cost. Buffett gave more details about the challenges, indicating that a major competitor, The State Farm, had refused to raise its prices.

- When asked why he chose not to repurchase Berkshire Hathaway shares even when they were quite cheap, he admitted that at one point or another in the past, he made a great mistake by not making repurchases. He admitted that his view of Berkshire's value at the time was too conservative or maybe he was too weary about other alternative use of funds. Therefore, they missed out on some great opportunities. Nonetheless, Buffett did make lots of money.

- He admitted that he made a mistake by paying what he

paid to acquire Dexter, a shoe company, in 1993. He admitted further by saying he compounded his mistake by using the Berkshire shares in payment.

- How about the Berkshire Hathaway textiles? Buffett said: "We made a major acquisition, we bought the Waumbec Mills, hoping that it will create greater synergy. But at the end of the day, it didn't work out as expected and I take the blame for not backing out sooner."

- Not long after acquiring Berkshire, he purchased a department store in Baltimore: Hochschild Kohn's. The store was purchased through Diversified Retailing, a company that later merged with Berkshire. Buffett was able to purchase the store at a substantial discount from the actual book value. The people involved were amazing and the transaction included some off-the-record bonuses — significant LIFO cushion and unrecorded real estate values with potential tax reduction. But how did he miss that? He admitted he was lucky to sell off the business about three years for about the same amount he purchased it.

- Sometime in late 1993, he sold about 10 million shares of Cap Cities at the rate of $63. But barely a year later, at the end of 1994, the price had grown to $851/4. If you do the math, the difference is about $222.5 million.

- Buffett admitted that the Cap Cities decision was a minor mistake compared to a major mistake he made in 1989 that later manifested in 1994. He bought the US Air preferred stock for about $358 million, on which the dividend was later suspended in September.

  He admitted the mistake by explaining that such lapse was due to sloppy analysis, probably because he felt they were buying from top security (because the owners of the preferred stock must be paid before the hubris or owners of common stocks).

- Another remarkable mistake he admitted to was purchasing the Gillette preferred rather than the Gillette common. He said, "I felt too smart to do that. If I had gone for the common rather than the preferred, we could have made over $625 million at the end of 1995 thereby making an 'excess' dividend of over $70 million."

Learning From Mistakes

If you fail to learn from your mistakes, it increases your chances of repeating the same or similar mistakes.

Regardless of any excuses you might have for making a

mistake, you still need to learn from the past, this will help you avoid making such mistakes, and that is an important part of learning.

Individuals who are able to face, analyze, and accept their mistakes tend to have a high level of self-confidence. These individuals know that though they make mistakes, they are still valuable, intelligent, and gifted individuals — and they are champions in their chosen fields despite their mistakes. In addition, these individuals have trained their minds to accept and endure the agony of self-criticism and the associated benefits.

Avoid Common Mistakes

There was a time when Buffett was asked to explain how he succeeded as an investor; he answered the question with a simple response: "I am rational." This is in sharp contrast with how most investors often responded thereby making the same illogical, silly, and emotional mistake.

A term that psychologists devised to describe the act of trying to convince yourself that your mistakes (which you're not aware of) is smart is called "stupidity." Another similar term commonly used is known as "recency." That is, trying to overemphasize a recent event. For instance, if there was a recent fire outbreak nearby, people around will suddenly start buying more homeowners' insurance; or if a stock keeps rising steadily, most people will start going after such stocks.

Just like any other psychological mistakes, recency could also serve an important purpose. Maybe fire outbreaks are becoming all too common these days or it is likely that these stocks will keep soaring higher because:

- some experienced investors are progressively purchasing big positions;

- maybe new investors keep discovering the stock. Often, they focus only on the recent purchases, rather than checking whether the stocks have been laying in a portfolio for years. Such mistakes could be quite costly.

"Extrapolation" is another keyword that is closely related to recency. It is the tendency for the human mind to accept that whatever happened in the past, will have to repeat itself repeatedly. For instance, the number that always comes after two, four, six, and eight is 10. Extrapolation could be a useful skill in life. A great restaurant deserves to be visited again; a good friend who gives helpful advice deserves to be consulted again. Things don't work that way when it comes to the stock market, however. A market or stock could suddenly become excessively expensive, and the number that will now come after two, four, six, and eight could be minus 14.

A sudden but significant event could have a multiplying impact on our way of reasoning or psyche. For example, a recent car accident could move us to purchase more vehicle insurance. Also, a recent fall in the stock market could cause us to lose a grip and result in panicking and selling off our stock.

Clearly, we investors are somehow a bunch of neurotic individuals. For example, many investors believe that they have no losses unless they sell off a losing stock on hand. Yet, there are others who believe that an individual bond is more preferred than a bond fund. Their reason? They believe that if you don't sell an individual bond before it matures, you cannot lose money (that's if it doesn't default before maturity). The truth is: An individual bond that is worth less than it should be will lead to loss even if you refuse to sell it.

The efficient market hypothesis has ironically been the most effective theory over the years. It's idea that stock prices are attractive and reasonable because all information is shared fast and equally, and that all investors are smart and logical. The Nutty Investor Theory matches this evidence better with idea that stock prices are either too low or too high simply because most investors are not logical.

In order to survive and succeed in the stock market just like Buffett, it is important to reject common psychological mistakes that most investors make.

The most common mistake is

extrapolation/saliency/recency, which could either drive the stock market down too low or shoot it up too high. David Dreman a value investor, noted in *Contrarian Investment Strategies*: "The primary thesis of this book is that investors overreact to sudden events. Overreaction is usually observed in our behavior, from the catcalling and booing of the local fans if the Chicago Bulls or any other great team loses some games consecutively or the loss of China and the outbreak of McCarthyism that will follow subsequently. All these are minor reactions compared with what is observed in the marketplace." (New York: Simon & Schuster, 1998).

Other popular psychological mistakes include:

- **Loss aversion**. No one loves to be at a loss and so, we all hate losses twice as much as we love winning. We all love betting on something where the odds could be two-to-one in our favor, but not the other way round. There are various experiments to prove that theory. Personally, I presented a case with similar odds to a group of investors: Assuming you overheard your company's chairman and the president talking about how great things are. The earnings are climbing; a major competitor is in trouble because of a new product that is flying off the shelves. What would you do, would you decide to buy more shares? Response: About half of the group said they wouldn't do so, while the other half said they would. Once again, I presented yet another question: Let's assume you own shares in a stock already and while you are in your company's cafeteria, you overhear the chairman and president lamenting bitterly about how bad things are. The earnings are dropping; a new product has overtaken the shelves and is flying around; a bigger company is crashing your dreams. What would you do, would you sell your stocks? Everyone in the group agreed to sell.

- **Love of gains**. Most investors are also likely to sell off too quickly, rather than selling their losers and allowing their winners ride, they retain their losers and sell their winners. Perhaps they're scared that their gains might simply disappear if they delay for too long.

- **The pathetic fallacy.** This word was coined by art critic John Ruskinan and it involves ascribing human qualities to inanimate objects. For instance, refusing to sell a stock because you were treated generously while working with a company or because a beloved relative gave it to you or because the stock was once a blessing to your pockets and now you feel indebted to it and worry that you will be viewed as an ungrateful person if you sell it. The safe truth is this: A stock doesn't know its owner. This is also called "personalization."

- **Separating money into different categories**. To explain this, let's assume the money you invested in stock from the U.S Steel has doubled, this motivates you to reinvest your profits more aggressively simply because it was easy money and not the money you worked hard for.

- **Cognitive dissonance**. Often, making certain changes in our decisions can be difficult and at times painful. For instance, substituting one set of ideology for another one. This may explain why many analysts are reluctant about downgrading a stock with a negative earnings surprise or slow when it comes to upgrading a stock that has a positive earnings surprise.

  Closely related to this is something called "endowment effect," which means that people readily accept any evidence that supports their ideas or beliefs (for example, a stock that they bought is a good buy) and readily object to any conflicting evidence that goes against whatever they believe (a stock they own is a bad one).

- **Avoidance of painful memories.** You carelessly sold stock and later regretted your actions, so it led you to believe that buying such stock again would bring back these sad feelings. Hence, you decided not to go for it even though the odds are great and could be in your favor. Personally, I always find it hard to buy a stock (or mutual fund) that once cost me money.

- **Contamination**. This is a fallacy of hasty generalization. For example, refusing to buy stocks or sell your stocks because of how a similar product in the industry is doing and thinking this product too might be affected sooner or later. This is not always the case, however, because a company in an industry could be more resilient than the rest, thereby benefiting maximally from the loses of its competitors.

Wise investors like to take advantage of such companies that seem to be immune against the sick industry. Recall how Buffett bought Wells Fargo at a time when banks were having trouble. This is also known as "false parallels." Around that period, some stocks flew up because they are in a buoyant industry, such as the Internet stocks, (although they too have some exceptions). This is known as the Halo Effect.

- **Complexity**. In some instances, even experienced investors get confused and don't know what to do. There are equally good reasons to purchase, as well as good reasons not to buy. I once had a conversation with Brian Posner, a money manager, who told me that he looks out for such complicated circumstances so he can gain an edge over other scared investors.

- **Top-of-the-head thinking.** There was a time when I heard that Pfizer Pharmaceuticals were in a big mess because they had manufactured a defective heart valve and that everyone who bought such valves might sue. I decided to sell all my 100 shares of the stock at $79. After the news had gone around, I watched as the prices began to nose-dive from $79-$72. Then, barely a year later, the price of Pfizer stock climbed to as high as $144. Seasoned investors will tell you that happiness is like a stock that can double within a year. The stock market is a world of "misery."

- **Thinking inside the box**. Most investors who have lost money on internet stocks often feel that they must get their money back by holding onto such stocks. As Buffett once said, however, it's not compulsory for you to get the money back the same way you lost it.

- **Anchoring**. In the stock market, everyone is searching for reliable guidance. If you just tell an investor the date when Armstrong landed on the moon, he can use that off-the-wall number as a guide to estimate the population of New York. In addition, investors tend to hold on to a stock's yearly high price. For instance, if they purchased a stock for as high as $50, they believe that selling it off at $25 is too cheap (especially those who follow the efficient market hypothesis). Therefore, they would prefer to wait until the price rises to $50 before they sell it.

- **The herd instinct**. At times, people prefer to follow the crowd or popular opinions, this includes experienced investors as well. One seasoned investor once told me that he will only buy stocks when there's an uptick. This is because often the voice of the majority is truly the voice of God. He went further to add, assuming I was in a cinema and everyone suddenly began running randomly towards the exits, I won't mind beating them to the door. Sadly, though, this theory doesn't work that way in the stock market. Often, the voice of the people is wrong. There are those who will always be stubborn enough not to follow the crowd, however. Indeed, there's a close association between stubbornness and courage.

- **Overconfidence**. Physicians, drivers, and lawyers, all believe that they are very skilled at diagnosing diseases, avoiding accidents, and winning cases. Such positive thoughts are often helpful especially when we apply for jobs in which we have no past experience. We enthusiastically undertake projects that are way above our head. Yet, overconfidence could also push an investor into taking too much risk, to trade too much, stubbornly refuse to sell, and to overestimate their knowledge.

- **The sunk cost fallacy.** People often pay good money for something bad. For example, if you've spent $600 trying to fix a car, it would be difficult for you to junk the car for a new one. But this will be not as painful as spending more money on the car. In the same vein, some investors are tempted to purchase more shares of stocks that had already gone down — probably to prove to themselves that they are wise enough not to buy it high.

- **Overlooking small expenses, especially if they are repeated**. Small expenses or small leaks, as Munger would like to say, end up sinking great warships. In their book, *Why Smart People Make Big Mistakes—And How to Correct Them* (New York: Simon & Schuster, 1999), Thomas Gilovich and Gary Belsky call this the "Bigness Bias." Or simply put, Americans often confuse grandeur with bigness.

- **The status quo bias**. Most people would prefer to do nothing than to do something that might later be seen as a mistake. Investors would feel happier retaining their stock and watch it lose up to half of its value than they would when selling off stock A and buying stock B, which will lose half of its value. This is backed by the common saying: From the frying pan and straight into the fire.

- **Confusing the case rate with the base rate**. If you examine a case, the solution may seem to be A; but if you examine other similar cases, you may find out that the common answer is B. A common example: In college, Nelly was interested in reading books. The question now is: Is she more likely to be a salesperson or a librarian? The answer: A salesperson, why? Because there are more salespeople in the US than there are librarians. In the same way, investors in the stock market may assume that a particular Internet stock would rake in a great deal of money without paying close attention to how many closely related Internet stocks fell.

- **Not distinguishing between what's important and what's trivial**. Reports from psychological tests show that when investors are well informed, they become more confident, but this doesn't make them better investors. Only the best-talented investors can separate the chaff from the wheat. During the Second World War, the US Army Intelligence was able to break the Japanese war code and began sending an overwhelming number of decoded messages to General George C. Marshall to the extent that he finally spoke out in frustration: Stop sending me unnecessary trivial messages.

Chapter 8: The Need To Plan

How do you think a journey you have not planned for will end? How about a business you have not taken time to think about, research, and draft a plan? In order to reach your desired destination, you must plan. Before venturing into a new line of business, make sure you do your homework, research about the business, and create a detailed plan. Planning is an essential tool for achieving goals.

Regardless of the importance of planning, many people, including investors, embark on a business journey without proper planning, especially when it comes to an investment policy statement. This is a statement that covers all your investment goals; the goals you wish to achieve, the diverse strategies you could employ to achieve the goals, and the various challenges you could face and how to overcome them. The reason most investors do not have detailed business guidelines and rules is that the outside world seems to play without rules and plans, including the media. You should know, however, that what works for them will not work for you, so make your plans, and forget what is practiced around you.

It is also very important to note that a plan is meant to help you make some very vital business decisions but at the same time, the decisions must be rational. Having goals is one thing, but achieving them is another, and execution is often the most difficult. Making business plans and setting up strategies does not mean the business will be risk-free or free of challenges, but it will help you to prepare for challenges and eventually make the right decisions should problems or issues arise.

A Financial Plan Must Be Alive

Since market conditions change daily, so should our business plan, investment policy statement, and financial plan — it should be constantly reviewed to suit the ever-changing market.

Once there is a major change in your assumed plans, the change should also be reflected in your investment policy statement and financial plans. There are some unplanned events in life such as death, promotion, divorce, and others. During such events, your IPS should be reviewed and changes made where necessary.

Apart from unfortunate and unplanned events, market changes can also result in changes in plans. In case of a bull market, which may suggest that you are moving too fast, ahead of your goals, you might want to increase your risk level if you are nowhere close to achieving your goals. You don't necessarily need to take more risks, but you could lower your future expectations (lower goals). This is not applicable in a bear market, however. The best policy is to re-examine the investment policy statement and its presumption on a regular base, preferably yearly. There are certain things you need to consider before writing or drafting an investment policy statement (IPS). These things include your financial status and other factors, which are:

1. The durability of your job;

2. Does the risk of your job correspond with the number of stocks in your custody?

3. The time duration for your investment to yield profits (investment horizon);

4. How ready are you to endure risk?

5. The necessity for emergency reserves.

Do not forget that your investment horizon can run from when you first invested until and even beyond your assumed retirement year. In some cases, it could extend beyond your death. This is usually if your investment plans covered your heirs.

It must be noted that a major requisite to taking risk is saving. Before making attempts to take a risk, ask yourself if you have saved enough. If the answer is no, then there is no reason to place the cart before the horse. Do the right thing first by saving as much as possible. As an investor, it is imperative for you to be able to distinguish between the strategy to get rich and the strategy to stay rich. While getting rich involves taking risks, staying rich comes with the ability to minimize risks, diversify such risks, and curtail excessive spending.

Another noteworthy point is that although a well-developed strategic plan is a must, your inability to incorporate it into your overall financial plan would render the whole plan incomplete. The said plan must include estate and tax planning issues. Other risk management issues that must be included are life, health, long-term care, disability, longevity insurance, and a lot more. Furthermore, your plan with regards to social security is of paramount importance. You must be sure of the appropriate time to start taking social security.

Lastly, you must have a detailed plan for your charitable ventures. Your objectives for wealth distribution to your family, including your kith and kin must also be taken care of. This can be included in your family wealth mission statement. Make sure you carry your children and their spouses (if any) along in your estate plan. Let them understand your intention of your plan before your death. The family's net worth must not be kept a secret from them. Also, introduce them to your financial advisors, attorneys, accountants, and any trustees entrusted with the execution of your will upon your death.

A contingency plan is another important issue that is worthy of consideration. Such a plan is needed to cushion the likely effects of failed expectations. Sometimes, your portfolio may fail to deliver the anticipated returns; such a plan would cater to that situation. Have a detailed plan of direction if the bearish direction of the market hinders your plan from being achieved. This would prevent your portfolio from running out of assets or all your goals from being unachieved.

Also, in your plan, ensure that you state the specific actions to take. For instance, delayed retirement or suspended retirement, if necessary, and reduction of expenses such as relocating to a low-cost house are specific goals that need to be clearly written.

Other specific goals to be include in your IPS are the planned increment you intend to make to your expenses every year, your asset accumulation strategy, including the dates you wish to achieve such goals, and the date to start withdrawing the returns from your portfolio. Ensure that you specify the amount you plan to withdraw every year. Taking these important steps will enable you to monitor your progress and make necessary adjustments.

After carefully taking the above steps, you need to specify your asset allocation or the makeup of your portfolio. This is the next step in developing your IPS. Ensure you make a detailed formal asset allocation table, stating the target allocation for every asset class with the rebalancing targets, identifying the minimum and maximum tolerance boundaries. A written IPS is important because it serves as a guideline. It also enhances self-discipline, a much needed trait toward the achievement of a goal. The next chapter gives a detailed way of developing your asset allocation plan.

Chapter 9: Diversification

In 1962, Warren Buffett was already popular with his profitable strategy, albeit with less risk than the average portfolio. While explaining his investing strategy to his clients, he revealed his consistent winning formula called "The Generals." According to the 1962 partnership letter, Buffett stated: "We usually have fairly large portions (5% to 10% of our total assets) in each of five or six generals, with smaller positions in another ten or fifteen."

Practically, Buffett's revelation shows that five or six stocks constituted 50% of his portfolio while spreading 30% among 10 to 15 stocks. The two main reasons for investing 80% of his total portfolio in about 20 total stocks during the said period were:

- Those stocks were very cheap and available;

- He diversified his portfolio by spreading it across different stocks.

Read his explanation below as regards his choice of stock:

"It is difficult at the time of purchase to know any compelling reason why they should appreciate at price. However, because of this lack of glamour or anything pending which might create immediate favorable market action, they are

available at very cheap prices. A lot of value can be obtained for the price paid. This substantial excess of value creates a comfortable margin of safety in each transaction." (Warren Buffet)

What Buffett is saying is that he focuses on stocks that are not on the "wanted" list of analysts and brokers. Such stocks are not recognized as hot stocks by the market, partly for the following reasons:

- No positive indication of the potential rise in price;

- The prices are too cheap for the market to see any potential;

- No new technology to boost the outlook of such stocks;

- No rapid rise in earnings.

As a result of the neglect of such stocks by most investors, supply far outweighs the demand. Hence, the price keeps falling because stockholders are selling more than buyers are willing to buy. Buffett comes in after spotting the right relationship between the value and the price of such stock. Meanwhile, the stock price may keep falling even after Buffett's purchase. This is because of the unavailability of any exciting event or fundamentals about the stock in question. This happens many times after he has bought a stock. The price keeps fluctuating.

"Just because something is cheap does not mean it is not going to go down. During abrupt downward movements in the market [these stocks] may very well go down percentage-wise just as much as the Dow." (Warren Buffet)

Diversification For Lower Risk

A reason to diversify in order to reduce the risk in one's portfolio is in Buffett's explanation below. He states:

"Combining this individual margin of safety coupled with a diversity of commitments creates a most attractive package of safety and appreciation potential." (Warren Buffet)

Buffett's definition of diversification, as implied in the quotation above is a portfolio comprising 50% in 5 stocks and another 30% in about 15 stocks. In contrast to what is obtainable in the contemporary world, such a portfolio would be regarded as overly focused and not diversified. It would surprise you that Buffett's strategy is something he still continues to use even today.

To Buffett, today's fund managers' practice of buying 100 stocks can best be regarded as "over-diversification." Such transactions are bound to result in negative returns that are even less than the average market returns if your fund manager's fees are added to the cost. Buffett's stance remains that concentrating one's money on only a few good companies that are on sale is the only way to consistently outperform the market. This is what he sees as investing. Any other means whereby amateur investors speculate and predict the potential direction of the market are mere exercises where they would eventually get their hands burnt.

The Folly Of Diversification

At the 1996 Berkshire Hathaway annual meeting of shareholders, Warren Buffett was asked by a member of the audience why there were only three stocks in Berkshire Hathaway's public equity portfolio. At first, he disclaimed the statement as untrue because there were other shareholdings in the portfolio of the conglomerate that was not worth reporting, hence, need not be revealed to investors. He later offered some enlightenment to the audience as stated below:

"You know, we think diversification - as practiced generally - makes very little sense for anyone that knows what they're doing. Diversification is protection against ignorance." (Warren Buffet)

He added that, "Nothing bad happens to you relative to the market" when you own everything. Such an approach to answering questions is appropriate for those who do not arrogate to themselves the knowledge of how to analyze businesses.

After offering a layman advice on diversification, Buffett turned to investors and analysts who deemed themselves worthy of business analysis and stock evaluation. He stated that:

"Diversification is crazy. And to have some super-wonderful business and then put money in number 30 on 35 on your list of attractiveness and forego putting more money into number one, just strikes Charlie and me as madness. And its conventional practice, and it may- you know if all you must achieve is average, it may preserve your job. But it's a confession, in our view, that you don't really understand the businesses that you own." (Warren Buffet)

Buffett stunned them by stating he could pick only two or three of the companies in the Berkshire Hathaway portfolio and dump the remaining. He would be content and happy to own and focus on such few stocks.

To many investors and fund managers, having a diversified portfolio of 50 companies or more is what is deemed acceptable. Contrary to their thoughts, the reality is that the world's wealthiest people have achieved their fortunes not through diversified portfolio but by concentrating their resources on only a few profitable ones.

In his reply to one of his shareholders, Buffett reiterated that only someone with a business eye can build a fortune.

Having said that, why haven't most investors invested in and diversified among companies like Coca-Cola? The first reason is that it is not easy to find such promising businesses. Moreover, only a few of such companies may be available for investors. If there were many, investors would capitalize on the opportunity and everyone would be smiling to the bank. The truth is you are not going to find such an opportunity.

One of the distinguishing features of a wonderful business is that it is formidable against economic volatility and downturn. It also survives stiff competition against its rivals. It is not easy to spot such businesses, but it is also not impossible. If you eventually spot them, there is more to what you can do than merely owning them as part of your whole diverse portfolio.

"But I can assure you that I would rather pick — if I had to bet the next 30 years on the fortunes of my family that would be dependent upon the income from a given group of businesses, I would rather pick three businesses from those we own than own a diversified group of 50." (Warren Buffet)

An average investor does not have such experience and may not be content with such few concentrated portfolios. Hence, the inability to exercise patience with few stocks as Warren Buffett did. Meanwhile, knowing and understanding Buffett's investment style and principles is an interesting and exciting experience.

Warren Buffett's Stock Portfolio

An interesting fact is that the same diversification strategy that worked for Buffett 50 years ago is what he still uses today.

The list of companies in which 75% of his portfolio is concentrated Coca-Cola Company (KO), International Business Machines Corporation (IBM), American Express (EXP), Wells Fargo & Co (WFC), Kraft Heinz Co. (KHC), and Phillips 66 (PSX).

To follow in the footsteps of Buffett, the acclaimed Oracle of Omaha, you might need to purchase about five good long-term stocks. Invest 50% of your money in such stocks. Thereafter, add smaller stocks to your positions. You need not shiver in case the price drops after you have already purchased the stocks. Rather, it may be an opportunity to buy such stock at a cheaper rate.

Should Buffett's Advice On Diversification Be Followed?

"Wide diversification is only meant for those who are ignorant of their investment strategy." (Warren Buffet)

Many investors have spoken up on the fouls of diversification. Among such investors, the successful Warren Buffett stands supreme and is a famous critique of a well-diversified portfolio. His aforementioned quote, which has gone viral, lays credence to this view.

Looking at billionaires like Jeff Bezos and Mark Zuckerberg, for example, it seems quite true that you only need to focus on limited business investments to get rich. In fact, it is safe to say that you need to exclusively engage in one distinct investment and master in that business enterprise. This ensures that your attention will not be diluted or spread thin, and all your focus and energy will be concentrated in that field. Be that as it may, a critical evaluation at this approach will reveal that there are numerous drawbacks inherent in the method of non-diversification. This method is far from being suited for everyone.

Survivorship Bias

Following the advice of famous investors and businesspeople often gives rise to the problem of survivorship bias.

Buffett's advice on how to invest has its strong points. Nevertheless, Charlie Munger will always remind us that the solution to any problem can be sought in the phrase: *"Be a contrarian investor; trade against the herd."* (Warren Buffet)

Quite sure, Buffett and a host of other popular and rich investors may have become rich by the approach of non-diversified investment. But recall that Buffett is one of the most committed, arduous, and intelligent stock analysts around who only invests when he is 100% sure of banging a profit. These qualities of Buffett give him an edge over 99.99% of other investors who can't boast the same level of commitment or level of intelligence. Thus, through research, Buffett can meaningfully reduce risk, a task too difficult for his fellow competitors to accomplish. They keep trying the same techniques all the time and yet, they expect a different result. On the contrary, Buffett and investors of his caliber always try new techniques, which no doubt bring a new, different, and better outcome.

A glance at the state of the Berkshire Hathaway conglomerate today will reveal that Buffett is probably more diversified than most other investors. Berkshire Hathaway's equity portfolio consists of more than 60 subsidiaries dealing in variety of products such as newspapers, railroads, utilities, insurance, jewelry and a lot more.

Today, Buffett benefits from the exact opposite of a concentrated portfolio; due to the fact that Dow Jones Industrial Average consists of only 30 stocks, Berkshire Hathaway is, therefore an index, apart from its equity holdings.

Buffett's sprawling empire is so diversified he generates wealth and profit from any industry he delves into. Certainly, this diversification has accounted for the group survival in financial crises and have also made them persistently healthy enough to bail out others. Had Buffett concentrated all his entire business in one sector, achieving this fit is impossible.

Net wealth concentration is one more vital factor to consider. Retirement savings is what the majority of investors tend to concentrate their investments on; this constitutes the bulk of the assets of an average investor. Giving his level of research and intelligence, Buffett has avoided such an approach and has thus been able to embrace a concentrated approach to investing. Buffett has always been able to spot the difference between investment capital and personal savings.

The average investor hardly puts the effort into research, unlike Buffett. This gives Buffett an upper hand against the average investor, whose significant loss would be far more destructive than the equivalent loss to Buffett.

When the market moves in your favor, add more to your position

Warren Buffett's advice to shun diversification is not suitable for every investor. One must personally work out a level of commitment. The efficiency of Warren Buffett's approach varies from individual to individual.

In summary, getting rich involves hard work and knowledge; it isn't all about money. Of course, Warren Buffett had $100 as his startup capital, which has resulted in a return of $30 billion.

Chapter 10: Risk Management

Practically all investors agree that investing involves risk. While investors all assent to the claim that investing involves risk, they also have diverse views when it comes to defining what risk is all about. In the common parlance, risk entails the probability of losing your capital. A permanent loss of capital is certainly disturbing because it spells danger.

So, to a long-term investor, what does risk entail?

For some, the risk is "Share Price Volatility." I beg to counter such view that risk in investment parlance is volatility.

Share prices are naturally irrational and more recently, computer algorithms easily drive share prices to absurd levels. No doubt this spells a degree of risk, but it is a risk that can be alleviated by two simple factors:

- Taking a long-term horizon on your investment portfolio. It makes no sense to try buying a stock in the morning only to sell it in the afternoon.

- Commanding a deep knowledge and details of the businesses you own.

These factors are evident in the life of Warren Buffett, who has over the past 60 years acquired a proven track record despite his experience of different market cycles, various technology changes, macro forces and geographical currents. His adoption of these factors has set him apart as unique and the envy of other investors.

Prevention

Buffett's method of risk management is quite simple. It is easy to implement but only for those who understand that it is more preventive than curative. Truly, the famous saying, "Prevention is better than cure," stands supreme here. Only the wise know and appreciate the importance of prevention. In business, only a few recognize this, and the rest give it little or no thought.

Buffett has not always had the best of ideas compared to his competitors. His outstanding secret is to always stay focused and avoid doing anything where he could lose a lot. Thus, he avoided a lot of things that could have pulled him back.

A great influence in the life of Buffett was Ben Graham's book, *The Intelligent Investor*. In this classic, Buffett learned his defining principle: That his shareholdings constitute only a small portion of his principal businesses. Consequently, there will be an improvement in the price of shares if the business is profitable. He pays a good price for the small units.

Share prices are often irrational, in the short term. To prevent this risk, Buffett with his long-term investment horizon focuses on long-term price movements rather than short term changes in price. Buffett has got the superfluity of permanent capital, a fact that makes him take a long-term view of his investments.

Risk, for Buffett, entails the possibility of harm or injury. For him, risk is intrinsically dependent on his time horizon for holding an asset. This means that it would be too risky a transaction to buy, for instance, a corporation in the morning and sell it off before the day ends. This is because Buffett thinks 50% of the time, one will likely suffer some harm or injury, unlike when you hold up the asset for a time horizon.

Buffett concentrates on business performance, rather than on market performance as it is directly proportional to the business performance.

Buffett's view on risk differs from popular thought, as well as the view in most business schools. The archetypal definition of risk in any common finance textbook is that risk is "share price volatility," unlike Buffett who sees heightened volatility as an opportunity. Buffett rejoices at the decline of share prices. This is because the majority of the companies listed in his portfolio are buying back their own stock. Hence, he adds to his future earnings from the company's returns without any hassle.

In business schools, volatility is viewed synonymous to risk;

an assumption that is apparently easy to teach but erroneous. Students and investors should be wary of such flawed teaching.

In the long run, Buffett views risk as "the permanent loss of purchasing power over the holding period."

Investment is thus risky not by beta (a term used in Wall Street to mean volatility and risk measurement gauge), but rather by the probability of an investment to reduce the purchasing power of the investor during the holding period.

Understand Your Investment

For Buffet, share prices don't dictate when he is wrong or right in an investment because he understands what he owns, and he knows what he's doing.

"Risk means lacking clear understanding of what you're doing." (Warren Buffet)

Business Risk

Buffett's objective is to own companies with potentially positive returns in the long run. Therefore, business risk serves as his primary concern. He always considers how his companies' earnings manifest themselves over time.

Buffett holds strongly that the risk involved in buying a company's share is not exclusive of the long-term risk evident in its business operations.

Buffett involves himself in business with low possibilities of risk. He thinks that the best solution to avert risk is to avoid too many risks.

The future outcome is a prerequisite consideration for Warren in embarking on any investment. He sees business risk as what could possibly happen in a few years that will erode, weaken or reduce the current economic strengths he observes in a business.

Buffett, just like every other investor, is not untouchable and is susceptible to mistakes. Of course, his failed attempt in companies like Dexter Shoes and Blue Stamps provide evidence of past follies. This failure is often because Buffett had misjudged the basic economic features of the business.

Filters, Base Rates, And Pattern Recognition

Over the years, Buffett has developed a rigorous and systematic approach of considering investments, which makes it easy for him to weed out investments of high risk. Buffett's aptness and knowledge in business have helped him identify potential risks and opportunities.

Filters

Buffett is concerned with being able to predict the future productivity of the business, which is why he utilizes his filters to evaluate the data available.

It is very important to note at this point that Buffett's "filters" are one of his most substantial risk mitigation and preventive measures.

Several filters have successfully been generated from his company. They don't promise the filters will capture every content put in it. They do not promise a 101% efficiency, but they too yield a positive result.

Buffett's first filtering principle is to comprehend what he possesses, and this is solely based on drawing a thin line on what he is knowledgeable about and what he doesn't know.

All businesses need to be at an advantage over their competitors, and it will be difficult to get one if you cannot comprehend the true meaning of business. It is usually more difficult if other people have a deeper knowledge of what it is.

It is important to operate within one's field of competence, we are all different people — each with our own unique business capabilities. There are many businesses and it is very pertinent to find the one you know best and can successfully run.

The importance of staying within one's field of competence cannot be overemphasized. If a prospective business lands beyond the circle and nothing can be done to get it in, he forgets about it. Buffett strictly abides by this and doesn't invest outside his field of competence.

Buffett's first deduction of any business would be to ponder on it, and he immediately determines if it's a business he can comprehend. If the answer is YES, next would be to determine if it can have a sustainable business advantage.

These filters are so effective, they can be used to make certain decisions in a few seconds and can reject as many as 90% of business ideas, which is sometimes upsetting to people who consult us for business.

Buffett does not lower the standard of his filters for any reason, they are exactly as described. He doesn't reduce or eliminate the risk involved to get a fat paycheck. If he projects into the business using his filter principle and can't predict the future of the business, it doesn't exactly mean the business is risky. It implies he simply doesn't know. The business might be risky to them at the moment, but may likely not be risky to another who is able to comprehend the business. Remember, we all have different business capabilities.

"Don't worry about risk the way it is taught at Wharton. Risk is a go/no / go signal for us. If it has risk, we just don't go

ahead." (Warren Buffet)

Base rates

This is one of Buffett's most productive filters used to mitigate risks. The overall percentage of pharmaceutical drugs that have successfully passed through screening to the percentage of the entire population trial is a good illustration of base rates. In this instance, the figures are few and not encouraging. Buffett has eradicated tons of potential business with a low base rate.

It is clear to Buffett that people with knowledge about individual cases seldom get the urge to know the details and the category the case falls under.

Baseline businesses, diminishing businesses, poor management, unreliable and unstable businesses, turnarounds, recent problems, low ROE businesses, and businesses with low prospects are instances of businesses Buffett termed "low base rate."

He doesn't engage in big trends and he does not get bothered about population trend because they don't account for much. They are time-consuming; it takes a lot of time to present themselves, there is a lot of money that can be made short term rather than the long wait.

Pattern Recognition

This is Buffett's main area of expertise and possibly his most substantial skill.

Buffett depends on a wide range of cognitive archives of data, which he utilizes to control risk. Buffett distinguishes himself by learning and pursuing knowledge without having to fill any need unlike the majority of people who only learn if there is a need to fill.

With his level of exposure and experiences to a wide range of businesses (their challenges and limitations) over the years, he is now able to effectively utilize the business experience and knowledge gathered to recognize possible business risk and failures in the nearest future.

In this case, having a reliable instinct is not in any way considered paranormal. It is called "pattern identification." With the right dose of exposure, experience, and knowledge, we can deduce patterns buried deep in our brain in a flash and remember complex details just like the thousands of chess positions professional chess players store in their collection. An adept professional would immediately perceive it when the pattern is wrong.

"Charlie and I have seen, and we're not remotely perfect at this, but we've seen patterns. Pattern recognition gets very important in evaluating humans and businesses. And, the

pattern recognition isn't 100% and none of the patterns exactly repeat themselves, but there are certain things in business and securities markets that we've seen over and over, that frequently come to a bad end, but frequently look extremely good in the short run." (Warren Buffet)

The business world, economy, and market environment cannot be predicted. Just like a gambler who sits at a pool table cannot be certain of his winnings for the night. They can be classified under a complex adaptive system.

One of Buffett's ways of countering this unpredictability is by creating a safety margin for his businesses. This connotes purchasing at a reduced rate to a cautiously calculated basic value which is why he persists on a safety margin in their procurement price.

He is convinced that this safety margin rule of Ben Graham is a fundamental part of a successful business. If by calculation, when the worth of common stock is somewhat a little higher than the procurement price, he wouldn't invest in it.

No Intolerable Outcomes

Buffett always looks before he leaps, he is always extra careful that even if a potential business has a high rate of success, he wouldn't venture into it if the aftermath to his portfolio would be negative. It doesn't matter how distant the potential threat on his portfolio is, a taint on his portfolio is inexcusable. He is very much willing to sacrifice a potential successful investment for a chance to sleep peacefully at night.

Think About Worst-Case Scenarios

You need to envision potential bad situations in your business to prevent unacceptable results. This is not something that comes to you in a spreadsheet, you must think and ponder on all possible directions the business is headed toward.

His perceives have not been susceptible to flaws that might hinder their power to participate as the right line of action.

He thinks carefully on every possible worst-case scenario and if they are presently indulging in anything that could end up a dreadful repercussions.

Buffett doesn't follow any guide to assessing risk but has his method to determine the risk and reward in every business they do. He doesn't think of what we learn in business schools as the true meaning of risk, neither does he trust the illogical fall and rise of shares.

He has always considered himself as a business owner instead of a stock owner. The fundamental law guiding this is that he is knowledgeable in the businesses he owns. If he doesn't have a deep knowledge of the business, then he certainly doesn't own the stocks.

Buffett goes further to reduce risk by steering clear of high-risk business such as IPOs. He isn't motivated with the huge return. He also avoids companies with high debt and low-profit rate.

Essentially, he is an individual with a wide range of experience and a reputable track record, which makes it impossible to disapprove his theories.

Buffet tries as much to evade investment risk with the help of the base rates, filtering and pattern recognition tools.

Chapter 11: Employing The Right Candidate

Employing the right set of people is important to a business. Many hiring managers have different ways of tracking down, screening, and employing potential candidates but what is most important is using the methods that have proven to be effective.

Warren Buffett is quite famous for his no-nonsense-strictly-business policy.

Warren Buffett's first principle when hiring someone is to employ the right candidate at the first trial. It is no surprise he employs only 20% of the candidates.

With this, he has established a perfect business model — one that enables rapid growth. Brilliance, vigor, intelligence, honesty, and energy are his hallmark for employing the right candidates.

Every employer has been hit with the scenario of believing that they have employed the best candidate, only to be disappointed later.

A potential employee who showed so much brilliance, knowledge, and conviction during the interview process — that they are the right person for the job — only to be employed and thereafter develop a pessimistic attitude, and exhibit an inability to solve problems independently, along with low productivity that directly affects the business especially after utilizing effort and resources on the employee. A new study by Ernst and Young claims one out of three team members disappoints their team as a result of low productivity.

A team strives with the inputs and efforts of each team member.

A disinterested team member whose mission doesn't align with the company's aims and objectives can significantly damage the business. Competent employees are the backbone of any business, which is why staffing and employment in any organization are of utmost importance.

Meanwhile, laying off such workers and employing new ones can be very unsettling for the company, especially if the company's hiring policy is defective. It will eventually lead to hiring more unsuitable people.

Many hiring managers have made the error of "mis-hiring," mostly as a result of the urge to fill a vacant position or a flaw in the hiring process.

The act of employing the wrong candidate can be cost-intensive to the company. The hiring process is one that improves with experience and knowledge. Take advantage of a few tips from a great mind in the business industry on the hiring process.

"Somebody once said that in looking for people to hire, you look for three qualities: integrity, intelligence, and energy. And if you don't have the first, the other two will kill you. You think about it; it's true. If you hire somebody without [integrity], you really want them to be dumb and lazy." (Warren Buffett)

The following are brilliant reasons why each potential employee should possess the above three qualities:

- **Low intelligence:** An employee with a high dose of energy and integrity with low intelligence quotient will turn out to be a loyal, honest, and active employee, but not a problem solver.

- **Low energy:** An employee with a high level of intelligence and integrity with no energy would not be proactive, which can reduce the company's productivity.

- **Low Integrity:** An employee with a high intelligence quotient and high energy but no integrity will turn out to be a smart-witted fellow who has no problem with stealing.

Integrity

Integrity is one of the three characteristics Buffett looks out for during the recruitment process. A person who doesn't have integrity would not be trustworthy. Obviously, when a person cannot be trusted, it influences every other area of his/her life and work is a primary aspect.

Irrespective of how rigorous the selection process is, all a recruiting manager can do is to process the picture the candidate has painted. The candidate has a deep role to play in this, they could paint a whole new personality and pretend to be someone they are not.

Therefore, the bigger the job, the more expansive the selection process should be from reference checks to thorough background scrutinization.

If a candidate is caught between lies, no matter how little, it is most certain there would be more lies. If this is the case, it can be assumed the candidate lacks integrity.

How do I know if a candidate is morally upright? Can I consider him/her a person of integrity? A sure way to shed more light on the issue is to apply Warren Buffett's "newspaper front-page test."

Assume that the potential candidate is called Fred. If media personnel gets access to Fred's work for your company and decides to publish their opinion of Fred, would you find it pleasant to read their thoughts of Fred?

If your answer is positive, then Fred might be an honest person but if you are still pondering on it, then you probably should let Fred go.

Intelligence

There are various types of intelligence; there is a thin line between emotional intelligence and smart intelligence. There is no clear definition of how to measure a person's intelligence rate. Intelligence may seem very easy to notice and at the same time could be very hard to notice. A crazy fellow may have the emotional intelligence quotient of a psychiatrist, while a genius may have the emotional intelligence quotient of a kid.

The first step is to identify what you desire in a candidate.

Hiring managers can adopt the use of aptitude tests, behavioral tests, puzzles, games, and interviews to determine the type of intelligence. As the selection process proceeds, create scenarios to test their problem-solving skills, creativity, and tactical planning.

Undiluted intelligence is essential.

Most times when people score high in a formal examination,

we tend to view it as academic intelligence, whereas it could be emotional intelligence.

Energy

It is very easy to identify an energetic person during an interview, from the personality to the gesture, countenance, and way of communicating. Being energetic doesn't have to do with how physically fit a candidate it, it has to do with the mental prowess. How can you handle the pressure? How can you deal with the demands of the job that may cause mental strain? Are you able to think objectively despite a long day?

A candidate who is energetic will be proactive, lively, optimistic, and have high endurance and the ability to withstand long hours.

A potential hire who is energetic would be enthusiastic and proactive when working. Exhibiting high energy also depends on passion. For instance, when you love something and you are passionate about it, you get excited and exhibit a lot of energy when doing it.

Energy And Intelligence Is Useless Without Integrity

Preferably, all three traits: integrity, intelligence, and energy should all be checked when interviewing a new hire, but there is one that outweighs the rest.

Why?

The rationale behind this statement is self-explanatory. If an employee has high energy and intelligence, but low integrity i.e., they can't be trustworthy — get ready for a financial collapse.

Case in point: Remember the story of Fred, Frederick Michaels; Now let's move Frederick from a hypothetical to a real person. Obviously, Frederick is a smart man — someone people highly admire. He equally has the energy and cleverness to convince people to let him be their finance manager and even clever enough, he is able to keep his past crimes that range over a decade, hidden. Cute right? Not really.

He defrauded many people, even people who were equally as smart as him. He was even able to fool big organizations like Yeshiva University Business School and Gift of Life Bone Marrow Foundation. I mean, one would presume they would have conducted apt interviews and didn't find him out. It is clear he was a hardworking, smart, and proactive man, yet dishonest and had no problem stealing.

To summarize, there are three qualities an employer should watch out for in a potential employee, but avoid an unnecessary headache, integrity should be number one on the list. Without integrity, the other two qualities do not matter.

We will all agree with Warren Buffett that there needs to be a blend of the three major qualities we look for in an employee (integrity, energy, and intelligence) for a company to be productive.

To improve the recruitment process, there is a need to consult previous hiring managers for counsel so we can avoid mistakes. In the process of selecting people to work together (from collaborators, employees, contract staff, vendors), whether they are clever, diligent, brilliant should not be the only criteria. We should also consider the most outweighing character trait, which is integrity. It serves as a determinant of business growth. If an employee fails in the other two qualities, it can be rectified, but if one is exposed as a dishonest person, it can do irreparable damage to the company on a long-term basis. If an employee of a company is labeled untrustworthy, then the whole company will be scrutinized under a microscopic lens.

Chapter 12: Should You Hire A Financial Advisor?

Whether the activity in question is domestic repairs or investments, there are two broad classes of people: Those who employ experts and those who would rather do things on their own, that is, those who are certain that they would do it just as well as the expert. It is sometimes better for those who belong to the latter category to employ the services of an expert. This is because when something is not done properly at first, it might be much more expensive to fix the mistakes than to employ the services of an expert. Another reason is that some financial mistakes might take a number of years to fix, whereas, others might even be permanent.

If you think you want to be an investor who would rather use your own skills, answer these five questions:

1. Do I have the analytical skills required? It is necessary to be knowledgeable outside basic math and have a comprehensive understanding of probability theory and statistics such as correlation and probability distribution, like kurtosis and skewness.

2. Am I knowledgeable enough to come up with an investment plan, incorporate it into a specific type of insurance plan — whether general tax, risk

management or estate -- then can I supply the continuing care and maintenance that is needed?

3. Am I solidly grounded in financial history? It is necessary to know how often the stocks have yielded a negative rerun, the length, and depth of bear markets. People who are not familiar with history have a higher chance of repeating previous mistakes.

4. While taking only the risk I am capable and ready to take, can I accurately determine the right asset allocation that gives me the highest chances of attaining my financial objectives? One essential aspect of the planning process is using the Monte Carlo simulator, an advanced retirement planning software, to evaluate the likelihood of attaining your financial objectives under different saving, spending, and asset allocation assumptions? Expected correlation among asset classes, expected return of asset classes, and expected standard deviation are some of the necessary assumptions to consider. The majority of this software can be readily accessed, although there are substantial defects in a lot of them. As a result of their intricacy, mistakes are unavoidable.

5. It is almost inevitable that I will be faced with crises; however, do I possess the mental discipline and disposition required to follow through with a plan? Am

I certain that I possess the doggedness to persevere in the event of a reduction in the value of my portfolio without being distressed? Will I be able to balance out my target allocations while also staying calm when every other person is panicking or purchasing additional stock even when it seems like the most unwise decision to take? Reflect on your feelings and attitude after the happenings of September 11, 2001, and during the period of the financial crisis that started in 2007. From experience, it has been discovered that fear results in a pause, or in worse scenarios, the apprehensive sale and desertion of well-structured plans. When faced with the loss of a bear market, even experienced investors are not spared from doing the wrong thing, this is because they become subject to their emotions which prevails over the trained action of their brain to do what is right.

This then causes what Carl Richards refers to this as "the behavior gap." This phrase describes the inability of investors to earn a return that is equal to the return earned by their invested funds. Reflect on these questions: Are my returns on par with my investments? Are all my actions geared toward the right thing? Are my action steps correct?

If you have scaled through this test, you are one of a very few. In addition to guiding you on the ways to build a portfolio that suits your specific circumstances, this book would also provide you with the highly effective techniques of making passive investments and global diversification. On the other hand, you might find out that you do not possess the discipline, temperament, or knowledge to attain success without external help. Even if you find out that you are qualified to do these on your own, you may discover that a solid financial advisory company can be helpful in a number of ways, such as creating additional time for you to concentrate on the most valuable things in your life, like periods spent with family, friends, doing relevant things. Therefore, time might be more valuable to you than the price paid for advice. All that matters is that you discover what works for you. If you choose to employ a financial advisory firm, this decision will be one of the most crucial choices you would ever make, because the outcomes will be life-changing. Therefore, it is of utmost importance that you do it well.

Chapter 13: Portfolio Management

The intrinsic value technique has always served as Warren Buffett's guide, whereby security is determined by the correlation between price and the value that the entire business would be bought by an experienced buyer. Still, there has been a significant transformation between the periods when Buffett left the security analysis class taught by Benjamin Graham at Columbia University and his present position as Berkshire Hathaway's CEO and Chairman. This transformation and constant learning have enabled Buffett to generate outcomes that are much more outstanding compared to that of other successful value investors.

The Early Warren Buffett

As of the late 50s when Buffett established the Buffett Partnership, his investment strategy was greatly influenced by that of Benjamin Graham, his teacher. It was based on the current value of the business, whether on assets, the financial records, or as a result of the earning power of a business with a solid history of similar outcomes. He learned from Graham that there had to be adequate protection against the future so that the previous foundation upon which the valuation of the company was built, is not impacted negatively by unpredictable events in the future.

He had a mixed portfolio comprising of what he referred to as "work-outs" (that included liquidations, sales, tenders, mergers, and other unique situations) and general situations where he enforced his authority over the company. Warren Buffett addressed a letter to his partners in 1960, these letters detailed the Saborn Map Company, which was the earliest major investment of the company. At its peak, it contributed almost 35% of assets. An overview of this situation shows that:

1. As a result of growing competition, there was a steep reduction in the profitability of the Saborn Map Company. The investment of stock and bonds at Saborn was valued at about $65 a share.

2. By paying about $44 for each share, Buffett was successful at acquiring substantial minority rights in the company.

3. He got on the Board of Directors by deploying his major stake in the company, and he was able to press for improvements that included demarcating the investment portfolio from other aspects of the business to estimate the actual value.

4. Eventually, he reached an agreement with the company, which allowed every shareholder who wanted an exchange of stock for their share of the

investment portfolio to go ahead with it.

5. This implied that stockholders who consented to the exchange were obligated to surrender their ownership of the notably depreciating map business; however, they were awarded a portfolio of securities valued at $65 a share, which could be sold on the open market.

In this scenario, Buffett was able to stimulate the growth of his investments. By applying a revolutionary approach, the value was unlocked within a short time frame. Bear in mind that this required him to leave some value available in the form of operating business, which he had to forfeit to reach a problem-free settlement.

Warren Buffett's Intangibles Phase

Prioritizing the intangible assets of a business was the next stage in Buffett's transition as an investor. Intellectual property, entrenched competitive positions, and brands are all referred to as intangibles.

On the other hand, tangible assets included equipment, property, and investments that were located in Buffett's previous investments.

There are two probable factors responsible for the transformation of Buffett in this manner. One was this friendship and subsequent partnership with Charlie Munger, who was known to deploy a technique that concentrated mainly on intangible assets compared to Buffett. Munger possibly made Buffett aware of the works of Phil Fisher, who described an investment strategy focused on a comprehensive analysis of the qualitative properties of business in his original work *Common Stocks and Uncommon Profits*.

The second possible cause of Buffett's transformation was likely caused by the scarcity of investments that had a considerable discount in their liquidation value. During Graham's era, it was quite easy to find a company trading less than two-thirds of adjusted net working capital (an estimation of the liquidation value of a business). Although after a while, these situations became difficult to find. In 1969, Buffett went back to his partner's capital, he attributed this to a shortage of interesting opportunities, he was probably open to new innovations to help him find better deals under this different situation.

See's Candy is a valid illustration of the investment from these times. In 1972, Berkshire Hathaway acquired this company (through Blue Chips Stamps, which was owned by Buffett and Charlie Munger). They paid $25 million, and the pre-tax earnings were below $5 million. This implied that at the corporate tax rate of 48% at the time, Buffett paid about 10 times more in post-tax profits for the business. Another viewpoint for this valuation is that his primary earnings were about 10%, which was a long way from the type of total returns he needed from his typical investments.

Although, See's Candy was a unique business with a major competitive advantage, or moat as Buffett chose to refer to it. In 2007, a letter was addressed to Berkshire Hathaway stockholders where he explained the investment proposition for the company and the outcomes that would follow.

Now you could see the radical change. Initially, the aim was to locate hard assets selling at a discount, and now, it shifted to the intangible assets of the company: its competitive potential and its capacity to yield extraordinary returns on prized capital. Accordingly, there could be an increase in the price paid relative to profits without diminishing the possibility of long-term returns.

In his initial years as an investor, Buffett would choose to pay very reduced multiple earnings that would result in a significant yield in initial earnings; by doing this, he was able to yield solid double-digit returns if the future roughly estimated the previous earnings record. An improvement in the companies that he invested in meant that he could cope with having a smaller yield in initial earnings since there was a high chance that these earnings would increase above inflation for an extended period.

Warren Buffett's 'Compounders' Phase

According to Buffett, it was almost impossible for a business that had a strong competitive advantage and the subsequent high return on capital to efficiently infuse capital back into the business at equal return rates. If that type of business model existed, it would be regarded as the ideal business: the strong competitive advantage with subsequent high returns on invested capital, along with an increased return on incremental capital that could then be re-channeled into the business. Therefore, a significant amount of capital that can be infused in the long run. This would result in a compounder, whereby a business could yield sustainably high returns and develop at unusual rates for a long time.

This is the type of potential that Warren Buffett saw in GEICO, the cost-effective auto-insurance company that he first knew about when he was 20. As in 1995, Berkshire Hathaway had ownership of 50% of the business, and plans were made to buy the remaining half for about $2.3 billion. Buffett regarded this as an unreasonably high price because it was more than two times the capital invested in the company.

Thinking back to the GEICO investment in his letter addressed to stockholders in Berkshire Hathaway in 2007, Buffett succeeded in buying a valid compounder that had a substantial competitive advantage and a high chance of profitability in the long run. In 1995, he became aware that this type of company came with a significant premium, compared to the value of any regular business. He did not mind paying some of that premium to facilitate the acquisition of an exceptional business lower than its intrinsic value. But superficially, it appeared that at the implied valuation statistic it was purchased at was quite expensive, according to the typical value investment standards.

Warren Buffett's Journey

His initial investments are a representation of this strategy — attempting to purchase already tangible assets at discounted prices. Through the years, he has transitioned into an exceptional business analyst. As his knowledge of business became more profound, he successfully progressed from purchasing inexpensive securities to purchasing excellent businesses that had a large discount to their intrinsic value, which assessed their future potential, which was projected to be significant improvements in the past records. In the absence of this transformation, it is possible that Buffett would have been successful. Despite the transformation, however, he has been extraordinarily successful. He has been able to widen his circle of competence — and it is necessary that we all do so if we desire outstanding success.

Chapter 14: Replicating Buffett's Long-Term Investment

This year, Berkshire Hathaway's annual letter was released to all its shareholders. It was revealed that the company hit its lowest annual profit since 2001. Buffett was seen on TV suggesting that long-term investment plans such as index funds are more reliable and can stand the test of time.

Buffett, who according to Forbes' estimation has a net worth of $84 billion, told CNBC that passive investments such as investing in an exchange-traded fund or mutual fund that tracks a major stock index such as the well-known benchmark S&P 500 (Standard & Poor's) are "logical and ever practical."

In that same letter, Buffett discusses his first investment of about $114.72 which he had been saving for many years and invested in a natural-gas company when he was just 11 years old.

He continues, "Assuming my $114.72 was invested in a no-fee S&P 500 index fund, and the entire dividends had been reinvested, then by January 31, 2019, my stake would be worth $606,811 (aside from taxes). Which would mean a gain of 5,288 for one."

While still on the interview with CNBC, Buffett told the

interviewer that supposing $10,000 was invested in an index fund of S&P 500 sometime in 1942, by now it would have increased its value to $51 million. The return indexes have grown so strong that Ted Weschler and Todd Combs two of Berkshire Hathaway's stock pickers, were unable to beat the S&P 500 according to recent reports. "Although, they are just a few figures behind the S&P, each, by nearly the same margin," Buffett said.

In the last quarter of 2018, Berkshire Hathaway recorded a $25 billion loss. Most of that money was lost due to an investment in Kraft Heinz. About $15.4 billion was spent on write-down on brands like Kraft and Oscar Mayer. Buffett admits that he was "wrong in a number of ways" about Kraft Heinz, such as the decision to "overpay" in order to acquire Kraft.

How To Be A Buy-And-Hold Expert

Warren Buffett was the pioneer of the famous buy-and-hold investing strategy. Although most of the modern-day investors in the fast-moving markets feel that the technique is already outdated and no longer applicable, the statistics tell a different story. The well-known investment company, Berkshire Hathaway (ticker: BRK.A, BRK.B), which is managed by Buffett, still buys stocks and applies the long-term philosophy of buying and holding stocks. From the records, there is no indication that suggests that the strategy no longer works: Berkshire's stock price has grown to 131% in the last decade, doubling the 65% return of the S&P 500 index. I must admit, it's not as easy as it sounds but if you carefully follow these nine steps, you would learn how to buy and hold stocks too.

Warren Buffett doesn't spend his money buying gold or other unproductive assets. He maintains three different groups of investments:

- **Productive assets:** This group is Buffett's favorite type, and involves investments that yield income and assets, provide services, and increase in value over time. Some examples are businesses such as real estate, stocks, and farmland.

- **Unproductive assets:** These include precious metals and cryptocurrencies. Although these items don't produce any goods or services or yield income, over time, they have the potential to increase in value.

- **Currency-denominated investments:** This includes investments in bonds, CDs, savings accounts and money market funds.

Clearly, things such as savings accounts and cash are not great investments because they are easily affected by inflation and could lose some value over time.

However, most investors are surprised when they learn that Buffett doesn't invest in gold. According to Buffett, gold, as well as other precious metals, are only worth something because we hope that they will be worth more after some time. In other words, their value is determined primarily by demand and supply, unlike other productive assets whose values are determined by their wealth creating ability.

"I have no views as to where it (gold) will be, but the one thing I can tell you is it won't do anything between now and then except look at you." (Warren Buffet)

Buffet doesn't rate cryptocurrencies. He sees them as just another group of unproductive assets. Apart from not producing anything, cryptocurrencies (such as the digital gold, bitcoin) are highly speculative and their values are determined crowd-rush.

While talking about bitcoin particularly, Buffett has advised, *"Stay away from it. It's simply a mirage. The belief that it has some large intrinsic value is just a joke."*

Warren Buffett Myths Debunked

In a bid to replicate Buffett's success, it is natural for people to attempt to know exactly how Buffett amassed his fortune. This popular speculation led to the circulation of various misinformation. As a result of such false information, many retail investors have been misled.

Listed below are four such pieces of misinformation, and why they're wrong:

Buffett doesn't invest in technology

Well, you can call Buffett old-fashioned, but reports have it that he doesn't own a mobile phone, nor does he have a computer at his desk. Rather, he stuck to his own (now-famous) advice on how to be rich: "Shut the doors. When others are greedy, be fearful. But be greedy when others are fearful."

Although most of us won't be willing to follow this advice, what is the best way to "shut the doors" and build your own opinions and silence the noise from your communicative devices? This doesn't mean that Buffett is unwilling to invest his fortune in technology, however. As it is his custom, he would never invest in any business he doesn't fully understand, a stance that is logical enough for any investor.

Let's talk about enterprise technology firm such as IBM, for instance. Presently, Berkshire holds about $15 billion stakes. Such holdings shouldn't be a surprise, given the fact that IBM trades at less than 15 times trailing earnings and forward estimates 12 times below, thereby repurchasing about $12 billion of its share price in previous years. Since 2008, this has resulted in an increased dividend of about 17% yearly.

Buffett doesn't like share buybacks

The truth is that Buffett only dislikes poorly executed buybacks, and he made this much clear in 2011 when Berkshire made it public that it is willing to pay 110% to buy back its shares.

Later in 2012, Buffett repurchased about $1.2 billion of Berkshire's Class A shares at around 116% of its actual book value, while simultaneously raising his limit 1.2 times. So, did such repurchase signal a failure of Buffett's age along with a reputation for identifying great investments? No.

As a matter of fact, Buffett proved this point when in 2011, he devoted a whole page of Berkshire's shareholder letter to declare his stance on stock repurchases. Whenever Charlie and Buffet want to go for any repurchases, two conditions must first be met:

1. The company must have enough funds to cater for the liquidity and operational needs of its business.

2. Its stock must be sold at a good discount when compared to the company's intrinsic value after calculation.

It feels as if Buffett sees Berkshire shares as really cheap, but he's back in profits if you consider the rising price of shares.

Buffett buys only cheap stocks

This assumption is especially hard to believe because Buffett is often quoted as saying: *"It's far better to buy a wonderful company at a fair price than a fair company at a wonderful price."*

By sticking to this principle, Buffett was able to build his empire, and this also helps to reaffirm the idea promoted by The Motley Fool, which states that winning businesses will likely keep on winning. This doesn't mean that Buffett is willing to buy a great business for any price, but when it comes to weighing risk vs reward, Buffett is the best call. At the end of the day, the overall quality of a business consistently supersedes its price.

In addition, this misconception becomes even more glaring every time Buffett acquires more businesses through Berkshire such as when Berkshire spent $26.3 billion to acquire the remaining shares of Burlington Northern at a 30% premium in 2009. Even more recently, Berkshire acquired Heinz at $23 billion at a 20% premium (to hit its all-time high).

In summary, Buffett deserves some credit for consistently demonstrating that he had what it takes to bring home the bounty.

Buffet hates dividends, and that's the reason Berkshire doesn't have any.

It is quite understandable if investors assume that Buffett

dislikes dividends. Besides, ever since he took over Berkshire, a dividend of $0.10 was paid per share just once and that was in 1967. In addition, Buffett once joked that "he was probably in the bathroom when the decision was made."

In his 2012 letter to shareholders, Buffett commented on this matter:

"Some of Berkshire shareholders including some of my close friends would like the idea of receiving cash dividend from Berkshire. Many of them wonder why Berkshire will enjoy the dividends it receives from most of the stocks it owns but choose not to pay out dividends themselves."

Yet, this doesn't mean that Buffett hates dividends. In fact, the reverse is the case. A long time ago, Buffett stated that dividends are one of four good ways to reward patient or long-term investors. At Berkshire, however, Buffett developed and uses an unrivaled capacity to develop an even greater value for his shareholders by combining the other three ways in acquisitions, share repurchases, and reinvesting capital in his business.

Having said that, Buffett has made it clear that Berkshire is willing to "re-examine [its] actions" if the day ever comes when Berkshire's dividend-free method repeatedly fails to provide enough long-term returns for its shareholders.

Chapter 15: Managing People

Looking at the diverse group of companies that Berkshire owns, one may wonder how Warren Buffett controls and leads such a company. Besides, it's the fifth largest company on the planet (Forbes Global, 2000).

Warren's Leadership Strategy

Over the years, Buffett has been employing a free reign (or laissez-faire) approach to manage his companies. This approach affords the employees an opportunity to carry out their tasks without much supervision or guidance from leaders. Much liberty is given to the employees to enable them to make wise decisions about what to do. In other words, each one is expected to solve his or her own problems.

While other employees in other organizations often have a senior member of the team who will be there to monitor their every move, this isn't the case for Warren Buffett. He always gives his employees a lot of liberty and leeway to make their own decisions. If you have any doubt about the efficiency of this approach, just look at how productive the company has turned out to be and what it has accomplished over the years.

The hands-off management style Buffett employs is based on the premise that people tend to perform best when granted autonomy.

Berkshire functions as a holding company and is used to purchase other companies. Some people, such as Shroeder, believe that Buffett's approach works because the firms he purchased already have experienced CEOs who are individually efficient and are profit-oriented. Simply put, Buffett stays out of the way and just lets them do what they are already good at doing.

Buffett's approach involves finding a balance between under-management and over-management. Over-management demoralizes talented workers while under-management leads to problems, especially when the leaders are not the best for the job.

The laissez-faire leadership style works efficiently at Berkshire because every company that was acquired already had its own culture.

Even though Buffett's approach has been successful, why have other leaders refused to follow suit? Schroeder explains: "The laissez-faire management approach is not for everyone. Special skills are required when applying it, especially in trying to hand things off and trust people to manage themselves."

Warren's Leadership Wisdom

The annual letter to shareholders of Berkshire Hathaway (Buffett's letters) is something most investors look out for. Most people dig into it in a bid to get investing tips, clues on who might succeed Buffett and to acquire wisdom regarding business and life generally. The 50th edition of the letter was released in 2015, and it contained information regarding the history of conglomerates and even some interesting stories such as how a giant root beer at Piccolo's can be made to float for dessert.

Buffett was known as the Sage of Omaha, the Wizard of Omaha or the Oracle of Omaha, Buffett is not scared of sharing his insights with whomever wishes to learn from his view on leadership and management. Here are some words of wisdom from his annual letter to shareholders:

- **Focus not on growing staff, but on growing the business.** In one of his letters, Buffett stated that a total number of Berkshire's employees went up over the previous year by 3%. But he noted that the increase didn't occur at the headquarters where only 25 people work.

- **Make sure the board members relate to shareholders.** One interesting thing at Berkshire is that board members are paid token fees instead of a huge sum of money for their role as directors. In addition, Berkshire's board set itself apart from other companies in that Berkshire doesn't protect their board members via the provision of liability insurance. In Warren Buffett's words: "At Berkshire, the directors walk in your shoes."

- **Benefits come from separating the Chairman and CEO role.** Buffett doesn't buy the idea of having one person serve as the Chairman and CEO at the same time. He desires that Howard, his son, succeed him as the non-executive chairman. With such arrangements in place, it would be easier to replace the CEO if things go wrong or when there's a need for the chairman to make some forceful decisions.

- **Don't permit arrogance, bureaucracy, and complacency.** Fighting off arrogance, bureaucracy, and complacency is a vital skill every leader needs. According to Buffett, if these three vices metastasize, "even the biggest and strongest of companies can fall." He went further to cite IBM, US Steel, General Motors, and Sears Roebuck as examples to make his point clear.

- **Trust is imperative.** Buffett chose to put his trust in the managers of the various companies owned by Berkshire. The trust that Buffett and Vice Chairman

(Charlie Munger) put on their managers has made it possible for them to achieve more "than they would have achieved by sending loads of directives, layers of bureaucracy and endless reviews."

- **Perhaps experience is still the best teacher.** In one of his letters, Buffett mentioned that two of his investment managers, Ted Weschler and Todd Combs will take on the management of one of the company's businesses. This role will help them become better investors via hands-on-the experience.

- **Admit mistakes and stay humble.** Buffett was never ashamed to admit that he "made a great mistake with this investment by wasting time" before selling off the Tesco shares. He also admits mentioning that some of his managers run the business better than he does.

- **Commend your employees.** Although the letter was addressed to his investors, Buffett seized the opportunity to praise his managers. Rather than use the collective "we," he mentioned the names of individuals. In addition, he didn't just stop at praising the managers, instead, Buffett went further to praise a former secretary who oversaw organizing the company's annual meetings.

Chapter 16: Maintaining Consistent, Persistent Results

"Success in investing doesn't correlate with I.Q. once you're above the level of 25. Once you have ordinary intelligence, what you need is the temperament to control the urges that get other people into trouble in investing." (Warren Buffet)

Although successful investing might prove difficult, it does not guarantee superhuman abilities. Like any other thing, investing successfully requires a gift that is uncommon: the capacity to recognize and defeat your personal psychological vulnerabilities.

Psychology has impacted our culture in various ways in the last 20 years. In recent times, it has significantly impacted the specialty of behavioral finance, resulting in many journals and academic papers that try to describe the reasons people make financial decisions that are of no benefit to them.

Behavioral finance professionals have a lot of knowledge to impart when it comes to understanding psychology and the attitude of investors, especially their errors. A greater aspect of the field is focused on deducing bigger trends of influence, for instance, the effect of human behavior on the market.

Winning The Game Of Life Stock Area Business

For many investors, stocks and the stock market are regarded as tiny bits of paper being exchanged between investors. This enables them to remain detached though it does not assist them in making the most effective investment decisions.

Therefore, Buffett said that he thinks that shareholders should regard themselves as "partial owners" of the business they are investing in. This helps to prevent investors from going overboard when making investment decisions, and they can rationally decide in the long run. In addition, longer-term "owners" are likely to extensively analyze situations. This meticulous analysis and thoughts usually result in a higher yield on investment returns.

Increase Your Investment

Although, it hardly ever seems logical for investors to "place all their investments in one place," it would also be illogical to make several investments in different places. Buffett postulates that not only is non-diversification bad for returns, but over-diversification is equally as bad. This is why he does not make mutual funds investments, and this is why he chooses to make substantial investments in just a few companies.

Buffett ardently believes that investors investigate diligently before making any security investment. After doing so, they will have the peace of mind to apportion a considerable quantity of assets to the stock in question. Also, their general investment portfolio should be limited to a few successful businesses with exceptional potential for growth.

Buffett's opinion on meticulous allocation of funds is reiterated by his statement that it goes beyond just the company, your feelings about the company is equally important. If the most successful business you own has the lowest financial risk and the highest potential for growth in the long run, is there any point in adding more money to your 30th favorite business rather than infusing that capital into the most successful business?

Reinvest Your Profits

Your return on investment is what makes your profit. For instance, advocating for something on a project that is approved and eventually yields positive outcomes. Accept the credit you just earned and become even more determined. Avoid asking for a raise or a promotion, simply continue doing the work efficiently. Re-channel that influence into the team or product. Concentrate on improving. Eventually, you will be rewarded; at that moment, simply keep reinforcing that credibility so that it can be efficiently utilized at the right time.

Reduce Portfolio Turnover

It can be extremely profitable to trade in and out of stocks, but Buffett believes that this type of trader is in fact impeding his investment returns. This is because portfolio turnover creates a price increase in the taxes paid on capital gains and it increases the cost of commission dollars that must be paid in a particular year.

The Investment Wizard also believes that what is regarded as reasonable in business should be viewed as reasonable in stocks as well. An investor should retain a small section of a successful business with the same doggedness that would be shown by the owner of that business.

It is necessary for investors to think long term. This mentality protects them from incurring large commission charges and high short-term capital gains taxes. They will be naturally inclined to withstand any short-term fluctuations and the business will eventually receive their rewards in the form of higher dividends and even earnings in the long run.

Have Alternative Benchmarks

Although stock prices are probably the standard measure of the success or failure of a particular investment choice, instead of prioritizing this unit of measurement, Buffett analyzes and comprehensively studies the intrinsic operations of a company or group of companies. If the company carries out all the necessary functions to help it grow and increase its profitability, there would be an eventual adjustment of the share prices.

It is important for successful investors to analyze the company they own and understand their true earning potential. There should be a noticeable improvement in the share prices in the long term as long as the foundation is strong, and the business is increasing shareholder value by producing steady bottom-line growth.

Think In Probabilities

Bridge is a card game where the best players can analyze mathematical probabilities to defeat other competitors. As expected, Buffett enjoys and actively plays bridge, then he deploys the strategies from the game into real investments.

Buffett contends that investors should concentrate on the operations of the businesses they own. Simply put, concentrate on the underlying businesses, then consider the probability that some events will occur or not, like the way a bridge player weighs the probabilities of other competitors' cards. He includes that an investor can accurately judge probability by concentrating on the economics of the business, rather than the stock prices. There are benefits to thinking in probabilities. For instance, an investor who weighs the probability that a business will record a growth rate in earnings within five or ten years is more inclined to withstand short-term fluctuations in stock prices. This implies that his investment returns are probably superior, and less cost is incurred from capital gains and/or transactions.

Never Suck Your Thumb

Avoid wasting time making decisions. Show precision and passion and be ready to make mistakes and make appropriate corrections. In the long run, it will be expensive to waste time on making decisions and it will reduce your ability to provide value to the people you are serving. Seth Godin's viewpoint on this is quite interesting, he advises capitalizing on commitments when others are still unaware.

Understand The Psychology

This implies that people must recognize that there is a psychological outlook that is required by successful investors. In particular, the successful investor concentrates on probabilities and economic issues. Rather than being led by emotions, he or she makes rational and logical decisions. More than anything else, emotions are the biggest enemies of most investors. Buffett believes that the secret to controlling your emotions is to maintain your beliefs in the actual principles of the business and avoid worrying about the stock market. It is important for investors to know that there is a mental outlook that is required for success and they should aim to imbibe that mental outlook.

Be Willing To Be Different

You are unique. In the whole universe, past and present, there can only be a single person that is you. Be prepared to just let go without any pretense and accept you have a special contribution to make. Nowadays, trends are unstable and certain people set trends for others to follow. In this situation, recognize your strengths and use them to set yourself apart. Exploit those strengths and set a limit. For a while, just concentrate on and discover your true self so that you can introduce us to your true self. Be you. Otherwise, you will feel inactive and depressed. Set a solid stance and set it where you are able to support your decision with proof and logical reasoning. The key to setting yourself apart is by building credibility.

Ignore Market Forecasts

There is a popular belief that the Dow "ascends up a wall of worry." Simply put, regardless of the pessimism in the market and those who constantly claim that a recession is "very close," the markets have progressed over time. So it is better to brush off the opinions of the pessimists.

On the other hand, an almost equal number of optimists

contend that there is a constant spike in the stock market. Their opinions should be disregarded as well.

Buffett contends that investors should strive to concentrate on segregating and investing in stocks that are presently not valued precisely by the market. The idea is that once the stock market starts recognizing the intrinsic value of the company (from the increased prices and higher demands), the investor is likely to make a significant profit.

Hold On For The Huge Pitch

Buffett advises that every investor should behave as if they have only 20 opportunities to invest. The idea behind this is that it should stop them from making inferior investment decisions and assuredly improve their portfolio's general returns.

Clarify The Deal before Starting It

Effective communication is important. Listen properly and confirm the problem again from your manager, customer or business analyst and ensure that your goals are aligned. As soon as you have done so, you can discuss the chances of success by clarifying your key success metrics. Creating a shared understanding of the initial phase of any process is very beneficial in providing a mutual feeling of purpose and encouragement.

Watch Small Expenses

Take note of all the details, without excluding anything. Carefully plan your work, be it designing interface programs, the taxonomy of your application or coming up with a story. Be meticulous in doing the work and put in the required attention to achieve a desirable outcome. This would help to increase your confidence, especially when you are discussing this with your clients or colleagues. Buffett kept breaking records, solidifying his spot as number one. This still boils down to his meticulousness, doggedness, and his perseverance in doing things in the proper manner.

Limit What You Borrow

Ensure that you fully comprehend debts and you smartly control them. If you are not familiar with the idea of design debt, Austin Knight provides an excellent explanation. Essentially, repetition and rapid cycles of release creates an environment where we just overlook everything. There is an increasing accumulation of all your excuses to "put that in mind and correct it in the future." Routine assessment of the benefits of your design strategies in helping the team or business attain its general objectives is a good way to eliminate the risk of debt mismanagement. You may just motivate a design restructuring. Use this method routinely in your product and design reviews. Here, the aim is to create a plan, avoid accumulating debts that may be difficult to handle, and discuss the position of the design debt.

Be Persistent

Even when things become hard, keep pushing. It might be insufficient technical resources, internal politics or complex design problems; be dedicated to the provision of value, and make sure to deliver. Despite the drawbacks, keep pushing through. Request feedback beforehand. To a certain extent, you will recognize what to improve upon in order to achieve better outcomes the next time you try.

Know When to Back Down

I could still recall some incidents that occurred during my career when I wish I could have backed down sooner, and most of those incidents occurred during a team's collaborative meeting or debate. At such moments, my focus was solely on defending and winning the argument rather than supporting my teammates and the product in question. I would get so carried away trying to ensure my project design was accepted by everyone, I would lose all sense of kindness (when I could have backed down and let it go). You can choose to defend your design principles for the whole day, but if it comes at the cost of hurting the feelings of your teammates, then you aren't doing it the right way. Always keep in mind that you're all on the same team, and the goal is to work together in order to achieve the desired outcome. Don't try to talk down your colleagues just to prove your point or defend your design. Trust me, no matter how good your designs are, there's nothing you can do to make up for all the hurtful words and bad attitudes you've shown towards your teammates.

Measure The Risks

Risk management is the bedrock of product design. It is important for you to assess areas where you have risk SSO, so you can be better prepared to mitigate such risks and predict possible outcomes. When you make some changes to a product, there may be a need for you to carry out some tests before pushing it out to the public so as to reduce the risk, and there are times when such tests are not needed. You need to know when to test and when not to. When you find it difficult to make decisions regarding a new feature or a change, it is better to speak up. Try to share your idea and fears (risks) with the rest of the team. By sharing ideas and brainstorming, the risks can be properly analyzed, and different suggestions can be proffered. Get a risk board and place it in an open place where people can easily see when engineering/sales/design/support is facing high anxiety due to risk. In addition, when a product is sent out into the market, try to monitor it and report back to other members of the team so that you can make the necessary adjustments and make some improvements on the product.

Experience What Success Really Means

At the end of the day, all the likes and retweets won't be able to bring about any changes. So, learn to appreciate the people around and take pride in what you do. Although, you may not be in the most attractive industry, and your customers may not be up to a million, your workmates are real individuals with feelings and many are facing various challenges. Try to get closer to them, invest in them, help them achieve their dreams, stand by their side when things are tough, and be sure to commend them for a job well done. In addition, learn to appreciate your managers because they are the ones who help you fight battles you never knew existed. And finally, always look for the good in men and women.

These little suggestions aren't taught in colleges, and that is why most young professionals enter the labor market armed only with the skills they need to protect and defend their career. Though I'm still a rookie in my career, I know with time, I'll be able to update and extend the list.

Warren Buffett's Favorite Way To Spend His Time

Surprisingly, Buffett doesn't spend his work days attending meetings, analyzing stocks, or watching the financial reports. Rather, he spends most of his time reading books. Buffett once said, "Often, I'll just sit in my office reading all day." He added, "You should read at least 500 pages every day. That's the best way to acquire knowledge. Just like compound interest, knowledge builds up. Everyone can do it, but I bet most of you won't do it."

Such manner of reading may sound like a big task, and sincerely, it is, but reading through some of the several investment books that Buffett recommended is worth the effort and it will help you get started.

Chapter 17: Foolish Investing Principles

Warren Buffet's success as an investor is widely acclaimed. Still, as Buffett has admitted, even the most experienced investors are not spared from making mistakes. The stories of Buffett's most costly investment mistakes are documented in the famous letters he wrote yearly to his stockholders at Berkshire Hathaway. Since Buffett's many years of experience as an investor are a rich source of lessons for us, I have decided to analyze three of Buffett's most costly mistakes.

Revenue Growth Isn't The Same As A Successful Business: The U.S. Air Case Study

In 1989, Buffett purchased preference shares in U.S. Air, undoubtedly convinced by the increase in revenue as at that moment. Instantly, there was a turnaround in the investment that became bad because the revenues attained by U.S. Air were insufficient to remit the dividends owed on his stock. Fortunately, Buffett successfully unloaded his shares at a profit. Despite his luck, Buffett became aware that this investment return was simply a stroke of luck and the positive expectations of people for the industry. However unbelievable it might appear, Buffett envies the small-time investor a great deal.

Moral Lesson

"Investors have poured money into a bottomless pit, attracted by growth when they should have been repelled by it." (Warren Buffet)

As highlighted by Buffett in his 2007 letter to Berkshire stockholders, sometimes businesses seem stable with respect to revenue growth, but huge capital investments are needed to facilitate this growth in the long run. This is what happens with airlines, usually more aircrafts are needed for a considerable increase in revenue. The downside of these business models that require extensive capital is that they will be immersed in debt by the time they yield substantial returns. Shareholders are left with almost nothing, increasing the possibility of the company going bankrupt in the event of a decline in business.

Buying At The Wrong Price Could Come Back To Haunt: The ConocoPhillips Case Study

In 2008, Buffett purchased a major stake in the shares of ConocoPhillips to benefit from the future energy prices. I believe that a lot of people might agree that there was a possibility that there would be a spike in oil prices in the long run, and that it is possible that this would be beneficial to

ConocoPhillips. Still, this proved to be a disastrous investment, because the price paid was too expensive and this caused a multi-billion-dollar loss to Berkshire. The price at which a stock was purchased is what distinguishes a successful business and a successful investment and, in this situation, Buffett could not have been more wrong as a barrel of crude oil was sold for more than $100, resulting in a rise in oil company stocks.

Moral Lesson

"When investing, pessimism is your friend, euphoria the enemy." (Warren Buffet)

Looking back, chances are that you would get carried away by the excitement of big rallies and ridiculously priced purchases. To carry out an unbiased analysis, it is necessary for investors to maintain control of their emotions. An investor who thinks rationally might be aware of the instability of crude oil prices and that oil companies have always been affected by bust and boom periods.

Sustainable Competitive Advantage Must Be Put Into Consideration When Considering The Company To Put Your Money In: The Dexter Shoes Case Study

Warren Buffett purchased Dexter Shoes in 1993. His

investment proved to be disastrous although the competitive advantage appeared stable initially, it waned almost instantly. Buffett says, "In just a few years, there was a quick dissipation of what I erroneously considered a stable competitive advantage." Stockholders lost about $3.5 billion and Buffett refers to this event as the biggest investment mistake he had ever made.

Moral Lesson

"A truly great business must have an enduring 'moat' that protects excellent returns on invested capital." (Warren Buffet)

A durable competitive advantage enables a company to earn high profits compared to other businesses in that location. Walmart sells at unbelievably low prices. Honda manufactures premium vehicles. As far as these companies can provide these things better than other firms, a high-profit margin is sustainable. Otherwise, other competitors are attracted to high profits, and they gradually chip off and extort all the profit.

Problems With Buffett Investment Strategies

Buffett's investment strategies have numerous shortcomings. The majority are due to investors begging for money or small investors. Usually, it is almost impossible for small investors to effectively utilize their strategies. This is mainly because they are unable to access management quality. Buffett has always had an advantage, even from his early years. Additionally, his mastery of investment was gained from trial and error, which is intolerable in real-life investment.

For a new investor, Buffett's investment strategies would result in failure. Failure can be attributed to the inaccessibility of the necessary information while Buffett had certified access to valid information.

Using Buffett's strategies means that they have to be altered to suit your individual situation with regards to the available information and financial position. For instance, more profits would be yielded by a small-time investor who chooses to invest a significant portion of the total funds in bonds and other profitable financial instruments. This is to provide regular returns and a specific degree of fund backup and eradication of risks. Therefore, there would be a reduction of the total earning in the long run since fewer people would possess these stocks; however, the risk of a complete decline in the portfolio is almost nonexistent.

Although it can be devastating to make financial errors, it is better imagined as the cost of learning. Proper assessment of your mistake and taking note of the lessons learned would possibly help recoup your losses. It is necessary for every investor, not excluding Warren Buffett, to be prepared for the unavoidable mistakes that would be made.

Conclusion

Chairman Berkshire and CEO Warren Buffett are considered to be exemplary models of the distinguished value-based investing method.

During Buffett's early days as a businessman, he said "I am 85% Benjamin Graham."

The fundamental value system originated from Graham. He is nicknamed the godfather of the value system (estimating the basic value of a stock to its future proceeding).

Subsequently, Buffett was able to refine the value system and followed a more intensive and standard approach.

Graham's approach was to identify and meet sub-standard and average companies and invest by becoming a stockholder of the companies while Buffett's approach is qualitative. He tends to invest in companies with an estimated projected future growth.

Buffett's fundamental value system principle looks easy, just like mathematical formulas that look simple, but the interpretation of the question would seem to be difficult.

To break the process down and interpret it easily, Buffett applies 12 business principles as a guide. These guides are based on business, management, financial, and value areas.

Buffett's principles may seem common and simple, but the application can be arduous. For instance, one of the principles seeks to know if the management is honest with stockholders.

Surprisingly, contrary to the principles that seem *easy* but difficult to accomplish, there are also principles that seem *difficult* but simple to accomplish. One such principle is the economic value added (EVA). Computing EVA is hard to understand and the explanation itself is complicated. EVA becomes easier when you view it as your market checklist that you make periodic changes to. Then it becomes simple to compute.

Business Principles

Buffett has maintained his resolution of limiting business to his "field of competence."

He believes his broad knowledge of the business will enable him to predict a feasible forecast of the business performance in the future.

If you can't fully comprehend the business, how would you be able to predict the business productivity?

During the 2000s tech bubble downfall, Buffett didn't invest in dotcom stocks, so he was not greatly affected.

Buffett's business principles encourage the fabrication of

solid and powerful predictions. The first step is to critically examine the business itself, not the market, economy or shareholder's opinions. The next step would be to check the archives of the potential business and check for coherent information, then use the information gathered to determine if the business has a long-term lucrative prospect.

Administration Principles

Buffett formulated three administration principles that are used to assess management standard. This is probably the most difficult logical task for an investor.

"Is management rational?" This was a question raised by Buffett.

He further asks, "Is management capable of reinvesting back into the business or remitting the agreed percentage of earnings to shareholders?" This question is deep-rooted as past surveys indicated that management can be insatiable and divert generated revenues to expand the business instead of using it to increase shareholder value.

One of the principles reviews the administration sincerity with the shareholders. Do they acknowledge when they are wrong?

Another question asked by Buffett is: "Can management withstand business imperatives?" This principle tends to look out for administrative teams that boycott rigorous activities and imitation of plans and schemes of business rivals. This principle helps you decide between wrongly imitating business rivals or outsmart them in an honest way.

Tenets In Financial Measures

Buffett's center of focus is on increasing the value of shares and return on equity (ROE) instead of profits. Anyone who studied finance should know that ROE can be greatly affected by leverage. If the company is a high leverage company, it might find it difficult to practice ROE.

Return on capital (ROC) is like return on assets (ROA) or return on capital employed (ROCE). Buffets clearly comprehends this and prefers to view "leverage" as a separate entity to equity. He is more inclined to companies with a low leverage record and high net sales.

Buffett's last two principles have a similarity with the conceptual basis of EVA.

"The residual equity theory assumes shareholders as the real owners of a business." Buffett is in full support of this theory as he also considers if a company can provide profits for its shareholders.

It can also be called "owner's earnings" or theoretically free cash flow to equity (FCFE).

Buffett interprets FCFE as net income + depreciation + amortization - capital expenditures (CAPX) - additional working capital (W/C) needs.

Value Principles

Buffett attempts to evaluate the basic value of a company. He predicts future profits, then compares them with the present.

You should remember that if you have used Buffett's other principles.

Buffett predicts future profits and productivity, and then applies them to the present. Remember that Buffett's other principles, the prediction of future profits would be simpler when you have a record of previous profits, they are easy to predict. He doesn't center his attention on the unstable present market value but on the future value.

The only exception for this is when it is going to benefit him. For instance, if a company's stable share price of $100 per unit of share suddenly fluctuates and hit $80 per unit, he would seize the opportunity and buy more.

The word "moat" originated from Buffett. Moat is the ability of a company to successfully maintain its edge over other companies preventing their infiltration into the marketplace.

The term "moat" has recently reemerged in "Morningstar's

successful habit of favoring companies with a wide economic moat."

Buffett asserts that the safety margin law applies to his predicting potential future profit. Stressing that the cautious application of his principles surmises that risk would be to a minimum or nonexistent at the least.

Bottom Line

In conclusion, Buffett's principles serve as an underlying basis for value investing that may require alteration and refining as time goes by.

It is unknown the rate of alterations that would be needed if long term operating data required to calculate future earnings aren't available.

The company's intangible asset is directly proportional to the franchise value and an unclear borderline makes it nearly impossible for extensive business evaluation.

Warren Buffet is a great role model for lots of people in the area of investing. Quite sadly, none has been able to follow in his footsteps. He recommends that upcoming investors purchase a low amount of S&P 500 index instead of an individual stock.

References

Buffett, M., & Clark, D. (1997). *Buffettology: The Previously Unexplained Techniques that Have Made Warren Buffett the World's Most Famous Investor*. Simon and Schuster.

Buffett, W. E. (1969). Letter to Partners. *May, 29*, 1969.

Buffett, W. (1982). Chairman's letter to shareholders. *Berkshire-Hathaway Annual Report*, 5.

Buffett, W. (1988). Chairman's letter to the shareholders of Berkshire Hathaway. *Inc. 2005 Annual Report*.

Buffett, W. (1990). Shareholders Letter. *Berkshire Hathaway, Inc. Annual Report*.

Buffett, W. (1993). Warren Buffett's Letters to Berkshire Shareholders. *Retrieved June, 13*, 2017.

Buffett, W. (1994). Letter to shareholders. *Berkshire Hathaway Annual Report*.

Buffett, W. (1999). Annual letter to shareholders. *Berkshire Hathaway Annual Report*.

Buffett, W. (2001). Chairman's letter, 2001.

Buffett, W. (2002). Berkshire Hathaway Annual

Report. *Berkshire Hathaway Chairman's Letter (21 Feb. 2003)*.

Buffett, W. (2002). Berkshire Hathaway Inc. *Shareholder Letter*.

Buffett, W. (2002). Berkshire Hathaway Shareholder Letter. *r~ w. berkshirehathaway, com/letters, html*.

Buffett, W. (2002). Chairman's letter. *Berkshire Hathaway 2002 Annual Report, 15*.

Buffett, W. (2003). Warren Buffett's Letters to Berkshire Shareholders 1977–2002.

Buffett, W. (2005). Letter to the shareholders of Berkshire Hathaway Inc.

Buffett, W. (2008). Letter to Berkshire Hathaway Shareholders.

Buffett, W. (2009). Letter to shareholders of Berkshire Hathaway. *Inc."(annual re*.

Buffett, W. (2012). Warren Buffett: Why stocks beat gold and bonds. *Fortune, February, 27*.

Buffett, W. (2013). Letter to Berkshire Hathaway, Inc.

Buffett, W., & Cunningham, L. A. (1998). *The Essays of Warren Buffett: Lessons for Corporate America*.

Cunningham Group.

Buffett, W., & Cunningham, L. A. (2001). *The essays of Warren Buffett: lessons for corporate America*. L. Cunningham.

Buffett, W., & Olson, M. (2013). *Berkshire Hathaway Letters to Shareholders 1965-2012*. Berkshire Hathaway.

Cunningham, L. A. (1997). Introduction to the Warren Buffett Symposium Papers. *Cardozo L. Rev.*, *19*, 221.

Drexler, K. M. (2007). Icons of Business: Jeff Bezos (Vol. 1). Greenwood Publishing Group.

Finkle, T. A. (2010). WARREN E. BUFFETT AND BERKSHIRE HATHAWAY, INC. *Journal of the International Academy for Case Studies*, *16*(5).

Gunther, M. (2009). Warren Buffet takes charge. *CNNMoney. com*, *13*, 2009.

Hagstrom, R. G., & da Serra Negra, A. C. (2006). *Warren Buffett*. Gestión 2000.

Loomis, C. (2013). *Tap Dancing to Work: Warren Buffett on Practically Everything, 1966-2013*. Penguin.

Miles, R. P. (2003). *The Warren Buffett CEO: Secrets from the Berkshire Hathaway Managers*. John Wiley & Sons.

www.ingramcontent.com/pod-product-compliance
Lightning Source LLC
Chambersburg PA
CBHW030638220526
45463CB00004B/1567